AUSTRALIAN PLANTS
for the Garden

GWEN ELLIOT is one of Australia's foremost writers on Australian native plants. She has written numerous books, the latest of which, *Gwen Elliot's Australian Garden* (Hyland House), has proved immensely popular. Her first book, *Australian Plants for Small Gardens and Containers* (Hyland House), was issued in 1979 and remains in print in a revised and updated edition entitled *The New Australian Plants for Small Gardens and Containers*.

Gwen and her husband Rodger have been involved in the specific field of Australian plant horticulture since the 1960s. All the plants included here have been grown by them, and the information provided comes from a background of many years of horticultural experience.

Gwen Elliot is an honorary life member of the Society for Growing Australian Plants, Victoria, and of the Arboretum Associates, University of California, Santa Cruz, USA.

Gwen claims that Rodger 'takes enough photographs for both of us', so we gratefully acknowledge Rodger's fine work, depicted in the photographs that accompany and complement the text.

Gwen Elliot with an Australian blue-tongue lizard, which is one of nature's pest controllers, with a healthy appetite for creatures such as snails.

Australian Plants for the Garden

GWEN ELLIOT

Photography by RODGER ELLIOT

Hyland  House

Contents

Frontispiece: *Dampiera linearis* and *Dampiera
rosmarinifolia*, pink form
Title page: *Acacia pycnantha*, Australia's floral
emblem

4

INTRODUCTION

Australia is renowned for its rich and diverse flora. We have over 25 000 native species and a huge range of garden hybrids and cultivars. While some of these plants are large trees, not suitable for inclusion in most home gardens, many are highly desirable smaller plants that are extremely attractive in foliage, flower or fruit.

The plants chosen here cover the full range of sizes. They include groundcovers, clump-forming plants, climbers, small to medium shrubs, and tall shrubs and trees. The flower colours include all the shades of the rainbow and flowering times cover the full year.

All are well tried in cultivation. Some are adaptable to a wide range of conditions while others are more specific in their requirements.

To gain the best results in our gardens it is important to give plants their preferred conditions; this information is included with each plant listed. Successful gardening usually means that plants with similar requirements for sun, shade, moisture and fertilisers are grouped together. It makes no difference whether they are all Australian plants or a mixture of native and introduced species: all can be successfully combined if their requirements are similar.

Many plants that look marvellous when young become large shrubs and trees and we should consider their eventual size when planning and planting our gardens. Too many large plants can result in an over-abundance of shade, and plants grown in close proximity to each other must often compete on rather unfavourable terms for moisture and nutrients. To help readers in countries where metric measurements are not widely used the approximate equivalents in imperial measurements follow in brackets.

Some dense planting may be desirable for shade and screening purposes but if it is possible to retain a relatively open area in the garden it will be here that you can establish some of the small and colourful plants that appreciate sunshine to stimulate their flower production.

Australian plants are often regarded as being ideal for low-maintenance gardens, and this can certainly be true in some situations. For those seeking a little extra in regard to plant beauty, a few hours spent from time to time in the garden can make a great deal of difference. Plants will generally be much happier if they do not need to compete with aggressive weeds. Most respond well to regular light pruning, and an application of slow-release, low-phosphorus fertiliser in spring may also encourage good growth and continued vigour. These aspects are all covered in the following pages.

Design and Plant Combinations

Good design is an important feature of every attractive, enjoyable and functional garden area, even though we may not necessarily have employed a professional designer or plotted the whole area on paper before planting.

It involves creating a series of living pictures within the garden,

Australian garden with *Dampiera linearis* (Common Dampiera) in foreground

considering foliage textures and shades as well as just the flowers, and planning a coordinated area rather than it being just a collection of different and unrelated plants. Good design also involves giving due consideration to the ultimate size of each plant and its preferred conditions for good growth in the garden.

A sense of unity in the garden can be achieved in a number of different ways. It is often done through the repeated use of particular plants or closely related plants that have similar characteristics of foliage or flower. It can be achieved through coordinating features such as pathways, mulching, lawn or grassed areas, through the use of logs or rocks, paved areas, or other landscape construction features.

It is of prime importance that the garden design and construction be functional. Any excess moisture should be channelled in the desired direction, through surface drains or underground agricultural drains. Erosion control that involves the elimination, or at least the slowing, of any water flow may be needed on steeply sloping sites. Provision must be made for easy access to all service areas on the property. The views to and from buildings are also an important aspect that unfortunately is often neglected in many garden designs. Items such as these must all be given careful thought and planning if we wish to avoid removing poorly placed trees and shrubs in the future.

The basic layout of a garden, and the selection and placement of large shrubs and trees, requires very careful planning and your efforts in this respect will be well rewarded in years to come.

When you reach the stage of selecting the smaller plants for the garden there is a wonderful range to choose from. Let your imagination play a major role in creating the garden you desire. Magic combinations may be obtained by letting shrubs and light climbers intermingle. The surprise of a Christmas Bell (*Blandfordia*) flower stalk emerging from the foliage and flowers of a *Brachyscome* can provide great pleasure, and delightful effects can be gained by placing the right plants together.

Attracting Native Birds and Butterflies

Gardens vary immensely in their style and function. Some involve mainly lawn areas with plants that are regularly clipped and rarely allowed to flower. Others have plants selected to include almost year-round flowering and they provide a constant source of food and enticement for birds, insects and other creatures.

Australia has a fascinating range of native birds, including colourful wrens, robins, pardalotes and other insect-eaters, honeyeaters both small and large which seek nectar from the flowers, rosellas and other members of the parrot family which are seed-eaters, and larger birds such as magpies and kookaburras which can be regular visitors to tall trees, on the lookout for grubs, caterpillars and other choice meaty creatures.

As well as adding interest and beauty to the garden, both through their colourful presence and often exciting flight and feeding activities, these native birds are also extremely useful in establishing a natural balance in the garden and in obviating the need for toxic sprays to control pests and diseases. Wrens and robins are well known for their insect-eating habits, while the nectar-eating honeyeaters can also consume several hundred insects per day in obtaining the protein that is also important in their diet.

We must provide three elements if we wish to attract

A kookaburra keeps watch near a garden pond

showy display featuring Flannel Flowers and Round-leaf Tea-tree

Melaleuca fulgens 'Salmon'

birds to our gardens: food, water and habitat plants.

Food can be provided by including nectar-rich plants such as species of *Banksia, Callistemon, Epacris, Grevillea, Hakea, Melaleuca* and others mentioned in the descriptions in this book. Plan your garden so that some plants are in flower throughout the year; this helps maintain a continuous natural food supply. Supplementary feeding can be used, in the form of bottled nectar and seed-feeders, but this should only be a supplement, not the major source of bird food in the garden.

Water in the garden is extremely important if we wish to entice native birds to the area. It can also provide much enjoyment as we watch the birds drinking, bathing or simply frolicking in the water. A bird bath, pond or any similar water source will be adequate. Water should not be in deep, steep-sided containers unless a rock, branch or other item is included so that small birds can enter and leave the water safely. It is also desirable that any water feature should be located in an area that does not put the birds at risk from your own or neighbourhood cats. A bird bath surrounded by a scattering of feathers is not a pretty sight!

The inclusion of some prickly plants for bird habitat will ensure that the birds have an area of safe refuge within the garden. It may even encourage them to nest in the shrub or safe thicket. If your garden has large trees, older trees with hollow limbs make ideal nesting sites for a wide range of species.

Butterflies provide an additional touch of colour and excitement to the garden during the warmer months of the year. These fascinating creatures are particularly attracted to daisy flowers, where the spreading petals and bracts act as visual enticements and landing platforms. *Pimelea* plants are regularly visited by butterflies during the sunny days of spring and summer.

Australian Plants for Cottage-style Gardens

There are several Australian plants that are ideally suited to cottage-style gardening. The long-flowering daisy plants from the *Brachyscome* range are excellent low shrubs, providing flowers almost non-stop throughout the

Brachyscome 'Mauve Delight' and 'White Delight'

year. Everlasting daisies from the genus *Bracteantha* are showy and long-lasting, while the small clustered *Chrysocephalum* everlastings give an ongoing display of golden-yellow blooms from early spring through to late autumn.

The Flannel Flower (*Actinotus helianthi*) has a fascinating display of creamy white daisies during spring to summer, and Kangaroo Paws are also well suited to cottage-style gardens.

Cottage-style gardens are usually free-flowering and therefore a regular supply of moisture and nutrients is important to maintain good growth and continuing flower production. Pruning is also essential to ensure that plants remain vigorous and attractive.

Fragrance in the Garden

Fragrance is another important aspect of gardening and here again there are many Australian plants with delightful fragrances.

Some plants have fragrant leaves, while in others it is the flowers that are perfumed.

Most *Boronia* species have aromatic foliage, while the Brown Boronia (*Boronia megastigma*) is widely known throughout the world for its beautiful and unique floral fragrance.

Other fragrant species listed in the following pages include *Darwinia citriodora* with spicy to lemon-scented leaves, *Eriostemon* species with aromatic foliage, Lemon-scented Gum (*Corymbia citriodora*), Native

Boronia megastigma 'Lutea'

Frangipani (*Hymenosporum flavum*) and Oval-leaf Mintbush (*Prostanthera ovalifolia*).

The benefit of fragrant foliage in the garden is enhanced if plants are grown near the edges of paths, where the foliage is brushed or can be touched by those who walk by, so the aroma can be enjoyed at close quarters.

Annuals and Short-term Plants

While many Australian plants are long-lived trees and shrubs there are also some annuals with a life span of one season only. Others are quick-growing, short-term plants with a life span of 2–5 years.

The fact that some plants have a limited life span is not necessarily detrimental, as they usually reach their mature size quickly and flower or fruit at a very early age.

Annuals and short-term plants are often included in cottage-style gardens. They can be extremely useful in newly planted areas while slower-growing long-term plants become established, or they can be used in rockeries and other garden areas.

Rhodanthe manglesii

Some Australian everlasting daisies or paper flowers are showy and floriferous annuals, including species of *Rhodanthe* (previously *Helipterum*).

The Flannel Flower (*Actinotus helianthi*) and Sturt's Desert Pea (*Swainsona formosa*) are not true annuals but in cultivation should be regarded as short-term plants.

Australian Plants as Cut-flowers

While most gardeners grow plants primarily for their beauty in the garden there are many species that give almost equal pleasure as cut-flowers for indoors.

Australia has many excellent long-lasting cut-flowers and several species are almost equally attractive fresh or dried.

A number of the plants listed in this publication are popular as cut-flowers, including Kangaroo Paws (*Anigozanthos* species), Banksias, Christmas Bells (*Blandfordia* species) Boronias, Gymea Lily (*Doryanthes excelsa*), Dryandras, *Eriostemon myoporoides*, *Hypocalymma angustifolia*, *Isopogon latifolius*, Mountain Daisy (*Ixodia achilleoides*), *Rhodanthe chlorocephala* subspecies *rosea*, Waratahs (*Telopea* species) and Feather Flowers (*Verticordia* species).

Further information on each of these plants can be found in the individual plant descriptions.

Growing Plants in Containers

The cultivation of plants in containers can be useful for those who have limited garden space or restricted physical ability. It also allows us to grow

Australian dried flowers

plants on paved areas, patios or in other situations where in-ground gardening is not possible, and can provide a successful method of cultivation for plants that are difficult to grow in the garden conditions of a particular area.

Plants have been grown in terracotta pots and large tubs for many years and this is still a very popular container type. Other materials used include a wide range of ceramic pots, both glazed or unglazed. Those that are glazed will lose less moisture through evaporation than those that are unglazed.

Plastic is an excellent material for container construction, being light in weight and fairly long-lasting. Light-coloured plastics tend to break down more readily than black or other dark colours. Timber is widely used, particularly for large containers such as planter boxes. Durable timbers such as red gum and jarrah are excellent and should be used in preference to non-durable timber, which will rot when exposed to moisture.

It is important that any containers should be large enough to provide a good root area for the plants being grown, with adequate drainage holes in the base.

A number of good quality potting mixes are now readily available and these should be used in preference to cheaper, inferior products. Most nurseries are able to provide helpful advice in this regard. A light

Lechenaultia formosa 'Pink'

application of slow-release fertiliser during spring to early summer is usually adequate to fulfil the plant's nutrient requirements, but a light top-up fertilising in late summer may also be helpful.

Container-grown plants should be watered regularly, as the root systems are unable to penetrate into the garden soil to fulfil the plant's need for moisture. The addition of soil-wetting compounds can be beneficial, particularly for moisture-loving plants or containers such as hanging baskets, which can dry out readily.

The selection of plants for container cultivation is of equal importance to the choosing of species for garden planting. There is the opportunity for exciting combinations of several plants in large tubs, or the grouping together of small or large containers in close proximity to create enchanting pictures with your container-grown plants.

Maintaining a Tip-top Garden

WATERING Knowing just when plants need watering is one of the most important yet often most difficult skills of gardening. There is unfortunately no fixed rule. The need for supplementary watering will depend on natural rainfall, whether the garden area is flat or sloping, your soil type and its moisture-retaining ability, whether the garden is sunny or shaded, and the plants being grown. We can however consider each aspect in an endeavour to provide the best growing conditions for our plants.

There is nothing we can do to affect natural rainfall levels, but in regions of low rainfall we can use contouring, mounding and small depressions throughout the garden, particularly near moisture-loving plants, to ensure maximum use of all the rainfall, rather than having it just run off in gutters or drains. Similar work is valuable if your garden is on a steeply sloping site, as it is important to slow down the flow of rainwater to avoid erosion of topsoil layers.

If you live in an area of high rainfall it is important to direct the water flow so that garden beds remain well-drained and are not inundated for long periods after heavy downpours. The building up of garden beds and the use of surface drainage channels or underground agricultural drains can help to achieve this. Alternatively you may wish to create a bog garden for the purpose of growing water-loving plants.

In situations where waterlogging of the soil occurs during certain times of the year, plants suited to such conditions will help to take up the excess moisture.

In well-drained to dry areas we can certainly influence the moisture-retaining ability of the soil through the addition of organic materials such as compost and leaf litter. The application of commercially available soil-wetting additives can also be beneficial. The use of organic mulches over

Colourful Australian native plants at Wartook Gardens, near Horsham, Victoria

the surface of the soil can assist, as these will gradually break down and be incorporated into the topsoil by earthworms and other creatures. Mulches also protect the soil from compaction and from direct sunshine, thus ensuring more favourable growing conditions for plant roots.

The amount of sunshine a garden receives will also influence the need for watering. Loss of moisture through evaporation will be much greater in sunny areas. In these conditions it is important to bear in mind that the best time for watering is during the early morning or in the cool of the evening, rather than during hot summer days.

Finally we come to perhaps the most important aspect: selecting appropriate plants for the various positions in our gardens. Some thrive in well-drained or even dry soils, while others must have constant moisture. Annuals and short-term plants are nearly always quick-growing and thirsty, while shrubs and trees have roots that can penetrate more deeply into the soil to find moisture and therefore need less assistance from the gardener.

All young plants will require regular watering until their root system becomes established in the garden. All plants should be given a thorough watering at the time of planting, and in well-drained soils it is valuable to fill the hole with water and allow it to drain before you actually plant.

Sometimes vigorously growing young plants will wilt during warm weather, not because the soil is dry but simply because the demands of the lush young growth exceed the rate at which the roots and stems are able to supply adequate moisture. Watering in these cases is often not needed, and plants frequently recover overnight.

Frequent light watering may be of use in regard to shallow-rooted annuals and herbaceous plants, but for trees and shrubs it is much better for them to have a less frequent but longer deep soak, using a low pressure or soaker hose or trickle watering system. This encourages root development into the lower levels of the soil rather than just near the surface, which is of course the first region to dry out.

Poking a finger down into the garden soil still remains one of the best methods of ascertaining whether watering is needed. Most plants will also let you know by their appearance whether they would like a drink. A sobering note is that more garden plants are killed by overwatering than by underwatering.

FERTILISING   Fertilising is another aspect of garden maintenance in which there is no one rule that applies to all plants. As with watering, annuals and short-term plants will usually need a much higher nutrient intake than long-term shrubs and trees.

The major elements required by plants are nitrogen (N), phosphorus (P) and potassium (K). Nitrogen is important for foliage development, but an excess could mean that plants do not flower as well as might otherwise be the case. Many Australian soils are low in natural phosphorus and the native plants have therefore become efficient in their use of this element. Excessive use of phosphorus-rich fertiliser can lead to an overdose, so several low-phosphorus Australian plant fertilisers are now obtainable to avoid this

problem. Phosphorus and potassium are the elements that encourage flowering and fruit production, and both are usually available in the soil in sufficient quantity for the needs of most long-term trees and shrubs.

Most Australian plants need only very modest amounts of fertilisers to maintain healthy growth and vigour. This can

Boronia heterophylla (Red Boronia)

usually be achieved by a light application of a slow-release fertiliser during spring, early summer or early autumn. In frost-prone areas the application of fertilisers during autumn can promote young growth that is then likely to be damaged by winter frosts.

Aged animal manures such as cow and horse manure can be used, and these also add useful organic matter to garden soils. You may need to be vigilant in regard to weed control if using manures such as these. Treated animal manures, which are basically weed-free, are also now available.

WEED CONTROL   Weeding is regarded by some gardeners as an enjoyable pastime, while for others it is an unwanted chore. Weeds are usually vigorous and adaptable plants which, if left unattended, can take over a garden, competing with or even eliminating favoured garden plants.

Some weed seeds are distributed by the wind, others by birds, and some we bring in ourselves with garden plants purchased or given to us by friends. Some weeds may be very attractive plants, but unless we want the garden to be overrun by those species they need to be removed.

If possible, young weeds should be removed as soon as they are noticed and before they get the chance to become well established and produce ripe seeds. In this way you will have little need for weedicides.

Mulches can be used to help deter weed growth but they should not be expected to eliminate weeds. In areas of bad infestation a weedicide may be necessary. Then a thick layer of newspaper, cardboard or woven mulchmat can be spread on the ground and covered with a more aesthetic layer: leaf litter, shredded leaves and branchlets, sawdust, coarse sand or other mulching material. Any weeds that develop in garden mulch can usually be removed with greater ease than from topsoil.

For weeds that can grow from even short sections of roots or underground tubers it is important to remove as much as possible of the entire weed without cultivating the ground and cutting the roots into numerous sections, each of which may then be able to develop into a new plant. The application of a weedicide may be needed to eliminate weeds of this type.

Grevillea 'Poorinda Royal Mantle'—a living mulch

Weed control is an ongoing maintenance task in every garden. It is something we can't escape, but we can make it as comfortable and enjoyable as possible. Obtain a pair of weeders' knee pads or a weeding mat, an efficient pronged weeding tool and a wide-brimmed hat for protection from the sun, and use the opportunity to become close to the particular area of the garden being weeded. There will often be birds, insects and other plants to distract you from the task at hand, but that's all part of the pleasure of gardening. You may even like to weed to the accompaniment of your favourite radio programme or recorded music.

PRUNING Pruning is another important aspect of garden maintenance if we wish to have healthy and attractive plants. It is a natural part of a plant's development. In the bush pruning is done by beetles, caterpillars and browsing animals, but in our gardens it is up to us to get busy with the secateurs. It is difficult to over-stress the importance of pruning plants from an early age.

Plants can be lightly pruned, right from the time of purchase and planting, to establish the desired basic framework, then repeated as necessary to maintain continued good growth and vigour. Generally, pruning will stimulate new growth and result in an increase of flowering in subsequent seasons.

Most Australian plants respond well to pruning after flowering, with the boronias and various species of Mint-bush (*Prostanthera*) growing much better when pruned each year; however, there are always some exceptions. Blue Hibiscus (*Alyogyne huegelii*) is one plant that can flower for most of the year, so pruning usually involves the cutting of flowering stems. This can also be an excellent form of pruning, as the cut stems can be used for decoration indoors. If you live in an area with cold winters, pruning in late autumn should be avoided as the soft new growth that is stimulated could be burnt by heavy frosts.

Pruning can be used to promote bushy growth, to thin out foliage so that there is additional light and air movement through the plant, or to control a plant's height or width. It can be useful to remove spent flower-heads or simply to tidy up unattractive sections of a plant. Pruning is also beneficial in helping to accentuate ornamental features, such as the beauty of a trunk, or pendulous branches and foliage. There are also some species that can be clipped and used for hedging, standards or topiary specimens. Examples are various species of the Lilly Pilly, including the Magenta Cherry (*Syzygium paniculatum*).

Pruning tools should always be both clean and sharp. Any plant sections that are damaged or diseased should be pruned away and the tools used should be dipped in a disinfectant before they are used for other healthy plants.

21

Light pinch-pruning can be undertaken with finger and thumb as you walk around the garden, without even the need to reach for secateurs.

PLANT PROBLEMS   Plants are sometimes affected by pests, diseases, and mineral deficiencies and excesses that detract from their general health and attractive appearance.

A good population of birds in the garden will help to control most leaf-chewing or sap-sucking pests. If we are able to find the offenders we can destroy them, or control them with low-toxicity contact sprays such as pyrethrum.

Bumps and lumps on leaves and stems can be caused by gall insects, which lay their eggs just below the plant surface. Control is difficult as the creatures are then protected by plant tissue, but the affected stems can be pruned and destroyed if you find them unattractive. Healthy, vigorous plants are not affected to a major extent by galls.

Sooty mould can develop on honeydew excreted by sap-sucking insects such as scale. It is also common for ants, which are attracted to the honeydew, to be present on affected plants. White oil or a solution of water with a mild detergent and contact insecticide will combat this problem.

Foliage discolouration is usually an indication of mineral deficiencies or excesses. A yellowing of new tips is often due to iron deficiency and can be corrected by an application of iron chelates. A yellowing of older foliage is a sign of nitrogen deficiency. This can be common in heavily mulched garden beds, where organic mulches can use nitrogen as they break down. Most garden fertilisers will provide sufficient nitrogen to remedy this problem.

An excess of phosphorus will usually be seen in a browning or blackening around the margin of the leaves. In this case a good deep watering may help to flush away some of the excess, but further fertiliser should certainly not be added.

Root aphids, weevils and root fungi may be of concern in some areas, and it is suggested that you seek advice from your local nursery if you suspect these problems are present.

Mulches should not be piled up around lower plant trunks and care should be taken to avoid damage to lower trunks from whipper snippers and other garden tools, as both actions can lead to problems such as collar rot or cut off the sap supply to the rest of the plant.

Australian plants will usually cope with most garden pests and diseases. Occasionally we will wish to provide some assistance, but generally it is preferable to replace the odd plant rather than to use toxic sprays regularly in our endeavour to maintain a healthy garden.

Anigozanthos 'Bush Ran

Acacia WATTLES

The wattle is Australia's floral emblem and it is therefore very appropriate that these are the first plants described in this book. There are over 700 different Australian wattles, and although many of them are small to large trees, there are others that are low shrubs or even groundcovers.

Acacia baileyana (Cootamundra Wattle) is undoubtedly one of the world's most spectacular trees when in flower during late winter to early spring. It is also very easily grown and we often take it for granted rather than marvelling at its beauty. The greyish green ferny leaves can be totally covered by the small but profuse golden-yellow flower-balls. The seeds provide food for native and introduced birds and this sometimes results in the development of young seedlings, so it is wise to avoid planting trees in areas adjacent to native bushland. There are selected forms of this species with purplish red or yellow new foliage tips, as well as a prostrate ground-covering form, and also a low shrubby selection.

Acacia boormanii (Snowy River Wattle) is another eye-catching plant when in full bloom. It grows to a shrub 3–5 m (10–16½ ft) tall with narrow green to greyish green foliage, and can sucker lightly to form a copse. Sprays of lightly fragrant, bright yellow flower-balls give a stunning

display during late winter to spring. Flowering can continue for a long period as the flowers are not badly affected by heavy rains, which can cause damage to other species.

Acacia podalyriifolia (Queensland Silver Wattle) is a very attractive, tall, shrubby plant, whether or not it is in flower. The foliage is silvery grey, with oblong leaf-like phyllodes. During late winter to spring its beauty is enhanced by sprays of bright golden-yellow flower-balls.

Acacia pycnantha (Golden Wattle) is the species now designated as the Australian floral emblem. It grows as a medium shrub or small tree and sprays of bright golden-yellow flower-balls provide an eye-catching display against the green leaves during late winter to spring.

All these wattles like fairly

Acacia baileyana

Acacia podalyriifolia

well-drained situations with partial or full sun, but with so many species to choose from there is almost an Australian *Acacia* for any situation. Most species are relatively quick-growing. Some can have a limited life span of up to 12 years, while others are long-lived trees, highly valued for timber production. It is important to keep in mind that quick-growing species can be extremely useful for particular garden situations, even if they do have a limited life span. They can provide rapid initial growth for screening or other purposes while the slower-growing, long-term plants become established. If we take the time to find out the attributes and requirements of the plants we are growing, we can then use this information to our own advantage in our gardens.

Acacia boormanii

Actinotus helianthi   FLANNEL FLOWER

The common name Flannel Flower provides an apt description for this plant, as the creamy white flowers are soft to touch, with a texture quite similar to flannel fabric. The greyish green, deeply lobed leaves are also soft and densely hairy.

Flannel Flowers bloom over a long period from late winter, through spring and summer and often into early autumn. They are excellent for use indoors as cut-flowers, and are valuable also for pressing and other craft purposes.

Actinotus helianthi is commonly a fairly upright, shrubby plant to about 1 m (40 in) tall, although some forms can be much lower. Plants respond well to pruning, or to the picking of the flowering stems. They like fairly well-drained soils and filtered sun or sun for part of the day. They will also do well in full sunshine although better growth will usually be achieved if the root area receives some protection from intense heat.

Flannel Flowers are ideal for inclusion in cottage-style garden plantings, particularly where a soft and informal effect is desired. They are excellent when combined with *Brachyscome* and *Scaevola* plants.

As the flowers reach maturity a cluster of seeds will form in the central area and these can be collected for future planting. Individual plants generally have a life span of 3–5 years, but there will often be a new young seedling in the garden to replace parent plants as they die, or you can assist the regeneration process by gathering and planting seeds as they mature.

This *Actinotus* is from New South Wales and Queensland. There are about 18 species, all native to Australia, including one that also extends to New Zealand. The majority of these plants have much smaller flower-heads than *Actinotus helianthi*.

Actinotus helianthi

Alyogyne huegelii   BLUE HIBISCUS

Blue Hibiscus is an attractive, evergreen shrub with bright green leaves, deeply divided into lobed segments. In nature plants are found in South Australia and Western Australia, but they are adaptable to a wide range of garden conditions in cultivation. A sunny situation is important for best flower production and plants generally prefer a well-drained situation.

From spring through to autumn they can provide a showy display with almost continuous production of their hibiscus-like flowers 7–10 cm (3–4 in) across. Several different selections are available, with flower colours ranging from white through light mauve to deep purple.

Blue Hibiscus can be a quick-growing shrub, particularly while young, and may grow to 3 m (10 ft) tall by a similar width. It responds extremely well to light or moderate pruning, right from the time of planting, and this can be important if you wish to promote bushy growth. Because of the plant's very long flowering period, pruning is not always easily done, as it usually involves removing some flower-buds. New buds will, however, quickly replace those removed, and the plant will benefit from pruning or from cutting some of the flowering stems for use indoors.

Alyogyne huegelii

Anigozanthos KANGAROO PAWS

Kangaroo Paws are extremely popular as garden plants and as fresh and dried cut-flowers.

These are clump-forming plants with narrow strap-like leaves up to 1 m (40 in) long. The tubular flowers, which resemble a kangaroo's paw, particularly when they are in bud, come in a wide range of colours, including shades of cream, yellow, orange, pink, red and green, or combinations of these. They have a dense covering of short, soft hairs and are produced on stems that may be 10 cm–2 m (4 in–6½ ft) tall, depending upon the species. In addition to the natural species, all of which occur in the south-western region of Western Australia, numerous hybrids are now available, some of which can produce flowers almost throughout the year. The peak flowering time is generally in late spring through to autumn.

The flowers of the Kangaroo Paw are rich in nectar and highly attractive to honey-eating birds. It is fascinating to watch the acrobatic displays of the birds as they drink the nectar while the flower-stems sway from side to side with the weight and movements of their feathered bodies.

Most Kangaroo Paws like a sunny situation with slightly moist but well-drained soils. If some of the flower-stems are removed by cutting

near the base as they mature, more flower-stems will be produced and plants will maintain healthy, vigorous growth. Older plants can be rejuvenated by lifting and dividing the clumps.

Anigozanthos flavidus (Tall Kangaroo Paw) is the most adaptable and easy to grow of all the Kangaroo Paws. It produces green, strap-like leaves in a clump about 1 m (40 in) tall by a similar width, and upright flower-spikes to 2 m (80 in) tall in spring to summer. Flower colour forms include yellowish green, pinkish red or orange–red. Because of the natural vigour of this species, numerous hybrids have *Anigozanthos flavidus* as one parent, in conjunction with another species of more eye-catching colour. Some excellent plants have resulted, including *Anigozanthos* 'Bush Ranger', which has bright red flowers (see illustration on page 23).

Anigozanthos flavidus

Anigozanthos manglesii (Red and Green Kangaroo Paw) is one of the most spectacular, and the floral emblem of Western Australia. The flower-stems are up to 1 m (40 in) tall and are densely covered in soft, rich red hairs that contrast vividly with the bright green to emerald flowers.

These plants like a sunny situation and must have good drainage. They are generally short-lived in their natural habitat and can be difficult to maintain for a long time in cultivation, but the floral display can be magnificent and more than compensates for a plant's short life. Hybrids of *Anigozanthos manglesii* with *Anigozanthos flavidus* are usually more adaptable and have a longer lifespan than *Anigozanthos manglesii*.

Anigozanthos manglesii

Backhousia citriodora　LEMON IRONWOOD

Of the world's many plants with a lemon fragrance, this is undoubtedly one of the most delightful. The leaves have a strong but very pleasant lemon scent which permeates the surroundings on a hot day or during heavy rain or hail. The fragrance is also released if the plant is brushed against, if the leaves are crushed, or if fresh or dried leaves fall to the ground and are walked upon.

Lemon Ironwood is a large shrub to small tree, which usually grows relatively slowly to about 4–6 m (13–20 ft) tall in garden conditions. Its beauty is enhanced by large clusters of small creamy white flowers, produced mainly in late summer.

Plants will grow in full or partial sun, preferring moist, well-drained soils. They appreciate protection from frosts, particularly when plants are very young.

The leaves of *Backhousia citriodora* are useful for fragrance in potpourri

and similar products. They can provide a refreshing lemon tea drink and can also be used like bay leaves to give a lemon fragrance when cooking. Dried leaves are obtainable, crushed or powdered, from Australian bush food suppliers.

Backhousia citriodora

Baeckea ramosissima   ROSY HEATH-MYRTLE

Baeckeas form a modest but very attractive group of plants in the Myrtle family. They are found in all states of Australia and have a lightly woody framework with small green, often aromatic leaves. Some are pleasantly myrtle-like and others are more specific with fragrances such as camphor or lemon. The small flowers can be very profuse during the main flowering period of spring to early summer, providing a delightful display in the garden.

Baeckea ramosissima occurs naturally in New South Wales, Victoria, Tasmania and South Australia and is adaptable to a wide range of conditions. It is a low spreading plant with some forms only growing to 10 cm (4 in) tall, while others can reach 1 m (40 in) high and spread to a similar width. Forms of this *Baeckea* which have been selected for cultivation have flower colours which include white, pale pink or deep pink and the flowers can be seen from late winter through to midsummer. Plants flower best if grown in a sunny situation, and they appreciate moist yet well-drained soils.

Baeckea ramosissima

31

Banksia BANKSIAS

Banksias were among the first plants to be discovered by European visitors to Australia, and they were subsequently named after Sir Joseph Banks, the botanist who sailed with Captain James Cook on the *Endeavour.*

This is certainly a most spectacular group of plants, occurring only in Australia, apart from one species that extends also to New Guinea. They are members of the worldwide Proteaceae family, to which many Australian and South African plants belong.

Each eye-catching flower-spike is made up of many small tubular flowers. They are showy in bud as well as when in flower and are excellent for cut-flower purposes, both fresh and dried. The flowers are followed by firm woody cones, some of which are prized for floral art or numerous craft purposes. They also contain the seeds from which further young plants are produced.

Most banksias, but particularly those from low-rainfall, sandy regions of Western Australia, grow best in sunny, well-drained situations. Eastern Australian species are tolerant of partial or filtered sun and heavier soils, but most still prefer good drainage.

Banksia coccinea

Banksia coccinea (Scarlet Banksia) is particularly well known as a spectacular and highly desirable cut-flower. Plants grow naturally in south-western Western Australia and the species is sometimes also known as the Albany Banksia. It is a relatively upright shrub 2–4 m (6½–13 ft) tall, producing grey and scarlet flower-spikes at the ends of the branches from late winter through to summer.

This species offers a challenge to many gardeners, as plants must have sandy or very well-drained soils in full or partial sun. They dislike high humidity and prolonged wet or overcast conditions.

Banksia ericifolia (Heath-leaved Banksia) is a showy and adaptable species occurring in coastal and near-coastal regions of New South Wales. Its flower-spikes, produced during autumn, winter

Banksia ericifolia

and spring, are 10–30 cm (4–12 in) long and are in shades of orange through to deep red. A selection that is cream with red styles is also available. Plants usually grow 5–7 m (16½–23 ft) tall, but some forms are of lower or more compact habit. Selected forms should be propagated from cuttings rather than seed, to ensure that the attributes of the parent plant are retained. Heath-leaved Banksia will grow in sun or semi-shade. Although able to withstand periods of waterlogging, a well-drained situation usually provides best results. The flowers are particularly attractive to honey-eating birds.

Banksia prionotes (Acorn Banksia) is most attractive when the soft grey buds just begin to open from the base to reveal the contrasting orange flowers. It is one of the Western Australian species that must have a sunny position with deep sandy soils for best results. Plants can grow 5–10 m (16½–33 ft) tall and the main flowering period is from mid-summer through to late winter.

Acorn Banksia is popular as a cut-flower, fresh or dried and sometimes dyed to produce a range of different, long-lasting colours. There are several Western Australian banksias with acorn-like flower-heads, all of which have similar cultivation requirements. These include *Banksia burdettii, Banksia menziesii, Banksia speciosa* and *Banksia victoriae*.

Banksia spinulosa (Hairpin Banksia) is a variable species from Queensland, New South Wales and Victoria. The most commonly grown form is a medium to tall shrub reaching 2–5 m (6½–16½ ft), but low, spreading selections are now also becoming popular as garden plants. Flowering is mainly in late summer, autumn and winter, with spikes 5–20 cm (2–8 in) long. The flowers can be lemon-yellow to deep golden-yellow, with yellow, red or purplish black styles. This banksia will grow well in most acidic soils,

Banksia prionotes

34

with a preference for good drainage. It can be grown in full or partial sun, and is highly bird-attracting.

There are about 70 different banksias, many of which are highly desirable garden plants. Some, for example *Banksia blechnifolia* (Fern-leaf Banksia), *Banksia petiolaris* and *Banksia repens* (Creeping Banksia), are spreading groundcovers. Others such as *Banksia integrifolia* (Coast Banksia) can grow as trees 15–20 m (50–66 ft) tall or may have both upright and groundcover forms.

Banksia spinulosa   *Banksia blechnifolia*

Bauera sessiliflora   SHOWY BAUERA

This *Bauera* is also often known as the Grampians Bauera, because it is in the Grampians Range of Victoria that these plants are found. They are shrubs 1.5–3 m (5–10 ft) tall by about the same width and they are usually found growing in the moist soils of sheltered gullies or forests. During spring there is a prolific and showy display of small, rosy pink to purplish pink open-petalled flowers extending along the stems.

This plant is relatively quick-growing and can be of open habit, but pruning from an early age will encourage dense, bushy growth. The bright to deep green leaves are in threes, opposite each other on the stems, giving the appearance of a whorl of six leaves surrounding the stem.

Showy Bauera will tolerate a sunny position but its preference is for filtered sunshine or sun for part of the day only. It is excellent for providing a bright splash of colour during spring in a moist and relatively shady situation in the garden. It will grow very happily in company with some of the shade-loving ferns.

There are just three species of *Bauera*, all native to Australia, and named after the renowned nineteenth-century botanical artists Francis and Ferdinand Bauer. *Bauera rubioides* is also very popular in cultivation.

Bauera sessiliflora

Blandfordia CHRISTMAS BELLS

There are four species of Australian Christmas Bells, found in Queensland, New South Wales and Tasmania. *Blandfordia grandiflora* and *Blandfordia nobilis* are the species most commonly cultivated.

They are small clump-forming members of the lily family, with waxy, usually orange–red to bright red bells tipped with yellow, produced on upright stems 50 cm–1 m (20–40 in) in height, in late spring and summer. There are also some selected forms with all-yellow flowers. Plants are extremely showy when in bloom, then blend with the understorey vegetation at other times of the year.

They grow best in moist, well-drained soils but are able to tolerate limited periods of waterlogging. A garden situation with full sun or partial sun will usually provide good results. Often patience is needed before the first flowers appear but they usually bloom readily in subsequent seasons.

Blandfordias have for many years been the subject of various arts and crafts depicting Australian native plants. They are excellent for use as cut-flowers but usually home gardeners prefer to leave them in the garden while flowering. Mass propagation projects are currently being undertaken with the aim of introducing Christmas Bells to the commercial cut-flower market.

Christmas Bells have evergreen clumps of grass-like leaves and it is important to ensure that they are not pulled out inadvertently when weeding the garden. Plants can be marked with a small stake or planted with other grass-like members of the lily or iris families where weeding is done with particular care.

Blandfordia grandiflora

Boronia BORONIAS

There are about 100 different boronias, all native to Australia with the exception of one that occurs in New Caledonia. The best known species is *Boronia megastigma* (Brown Boronia), which is highly prized for its exquisite floral fragrance; however, the majority of species have pale to deep pink flowers and a range of different fragrances in flower and foliage.

Boronias generally prefer moist but well-drained soils and a relatively cool root area. Most like filtered sun or sun for part of the day only, while some will grow and flower well in sites that receive no direct sunshine at all. Those that do well in full sunshine usually appreciate some protection for their root system.

All boronias respond well to pruning after flowering, and the removal of one-third to half of the length of the leafy stems is appropriate. Plants can also be pruned by cutting during the flowering period; this enables

Boronia heterophylla

the stems to be used for cut-flowers. Many are grown commercially for this purpose.

Boronia heterophylla (Red Boronia) is widely grown for cut-flower production, both in Australia and overseas. It flowers mainly in late winter to spring, with a profuse display of bright reddish pink, lightly fragrant bell-like flowers to 1 cm (¼ in) long. Plants grow well in filtered or partial sun and can reach 2–3 m (6½–10 ft) in height. They should be lightly pruned from an early age to establish bushy growth, then pruned each year during or after flowering to maintain healthy, vigorous growth. The flowers usually retain their rich colour when dried or pressed.

Boronia megastigma (Brown Boronia) is a very well known species, grown commercially for cut-flower production and for the delightful fragrance of the flowers. They are commonly light to dark brown or burgundy with a yellowish interior to the small pendent cups, but selections are available with yellowish green or striped flowers. Plants usually grow 1–1.5 m (3¼–5 ft) tall and can have a life span of 20 years or more, but they will not survive if the root system is allowed to dry out and many cultivated plants are lost for this reason. Pruning is also important for maintaining healthy and vigorous plants (see *Boronia heterophylla*, above).

Boronia megastigma 'Jack Maguire's Red'

Boronia muelleri 'Sunset Serenade' is probably the most widely grown form of *Boronia muelleri*. It is a densely foliaged shrub about 1 m (40 in) tall and 1 m (40 in) wide with aromatic green leaves. During spring there is an eye-catching display of 4-petalled, starry, pale pink flowers that can almost cover the foliage.

This boronia will grow and flower well in light to fairly heavy shade. It can also be grown in positions receiving morning sun or full sun for part of the day. It likes moist yet well-drained soil.

Boronia muelleri 'Sunset Serenade' is also suitable for container cultivation in a medium-sized pot 30–45 cm (12–18 in) in diameter.

This species was named in honour of Baron Sir Ferdinand von Mueller, the first Government Botanist of Victoria. Plants are found in native forest areas of New South Wales and Victoria, where some forms can grow up to 6 m (20 ft) tall.

Boronia pinnata (Pinnate or Fern-leaf Boronia) is one of the many boronias with open-petalled, somewhat starry pink flowers. The leaves are divided into 5–9 small leaflets and they have a pleasant camphor fragrance. Plants will grow in partial to full sunshine but prefer some protection, particularly for the root area. They respond well to pruning during or after flowering. A white-flowered selection is becoming increasingly popular in cultivation and the white and pink forms can look superb when planted together. A double-flowered form of this species is sometimes available from nurseries.

Most boronia flowers retain much of their colour and fragrance when pressed or dried and are useful in pot pourri and for numerous craft purposes. You might like to look for other boronias at specialist native plant nurseries, as many are excellent for cultivation in gardens or containers if given their preferred growing conditions.

Brachyscome DAISIES

Brachyscome daisies are native to Australia, New Guinea and New Zealand. There are about 100 species, with further botanical research still being undertaken. Several are commonly cultivated, both in Australia and overseas, with numerous named cultivars obtainable.

Brachyscome multifida (Cut-leaf Daisy) is an extremely attractive small plant with a bonus in that many forms can provide year-round flowering. The soft flowers are usually 1–2 cm (¼–¾ in) across and colour forms include white, pink, pale to bright blue or soft mauve to reddish purple, all with a yellow centre.

Plants can vary from being compact and only about 10 cm (4 in) tall, to almost 50 cm (20 in) tall by 1 m (40 in) across. They are excellent for planting in well-drained garden situations or for containers and hanging baskets. They will grow in full open sunshine, and also do well in filtered or partial sun.

Brachyscomes respond well to pruning, which can be done throughout the year, but it is usually most successful during late summer to early autumn after they have been in flower for some months and when new bushy growth will be stimulated. If desired, it can be done again in late winter to early spring.

Brachyscome multifida 'Breakoday'

Named cultivars of Cut-leaf Daisy include *Brachyscome multifida* 'Breakoday', which has rich bluish purple flowers, and *Brachyscome multifida* 'White Delight', which is a moderately compact selection with white flowers on slender, erect stems.

Hybrids with *Brachyscome multifida* as one of the parents include *Brachyscome* 'Lemon Twist', which has lemon-yellow flowers, and *Brachyscome* 'Mauve Delight', with attractive soft mauve flowers.

Other *Brachyscome* that will provide much pleasure include *Brachyscome segmentosa*, with moderately large white flowers, and *Brachyscome* 'Strawberry Mousse', which has lovely mauve–pink daisies.

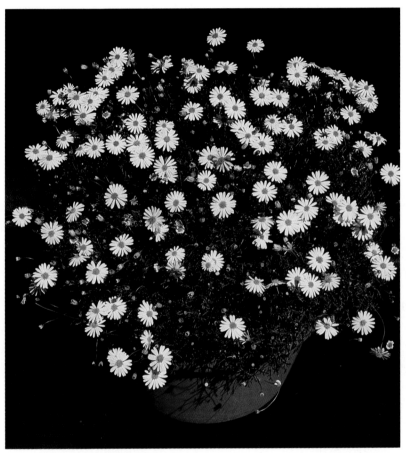

Brachyscome multifida 'White Delight'

Bracteantha bracteata   EVERLASTINGS

There is now a wide range of plants available within this species, which was until recently known as *Helichrysum bracteatum*. All have showy, stiff, papery everlasting daisy flower-heads that are produced through most of the year, with a peak from spring through to late autumn.

Named selections of Everlastings include *Bracteantha bracteata* 'Dargan Hill Monarch', 'Golden Bowerbird' and 'Princess of Wales', which are all bushy shrubs to 1 m (3¼ ft) tall by a similar width, with bright golden-yellow flower-heads. *Bracteantha bracteata* 'Cockatoo' and 'Lemon Monarch' have lemon-yellow flowers, 'White Monarch' has white bracts with a yellow centre, and the flowers of 'Spectrum' are a deep to dusky pink.

Bracteantha bracteata 'Diamond Head' is a ground-covering selection with golden-yellow flower-heads on short upright stems, while 'Gold 'n' Bronze' is a low, spreading plant with golden flowers surrounded by papery bronze bracts, produced above the foliage on erect stems about 30 cm (1 ft) tall.

The above are all evergreen perennial plants with a lifespan of 3–5 years, but there are some annual and biennial forms. All are extremely showy and well worth growing in small or large gardens.

Bracteantha bracteata 'Dargan Hill Monarch'

Everlastings are very long-flowering plants that like a sunny situation with moist but well-drained soils. The effort put into growth and flower production results in their needing a regular supply of moisture and they can be among the first plants to wilt in the garden if the soil dries out. They respond well to light applications of slow-release fertiliser in early spring and again in early autumn.

Regular pruning, or picking of the flowers, encourages bushy growth and production of new blooms. Do not hesitate to be a bold pruner of these plants. The flowers are excellent for use indoors and retain their beauty when dried if they are picked fairly soon after the buds mature and the daisies open. Flowering stems can be hung upside down when drying to ensure the stems dry straight, or the flower-heads can be removed and the stems replaced with florists' wire.

Everlastings are excellent for all who like year-round colour in the garden. They strike readily from cuttings, so you can replace older plants as they begin to lose their vigour. They are ideal for inclusion in cottage-style gardens and also for attracting butterflies to the garden. They are also excellent for providing quick results in a newly planted garden.

Bracteantha bracteata 'Gold 'n' Bronze'

Callistemon BOTTLEBRUSHES

Callistemons are extremely useful plants in the garden, as many are able to tolerate a wide range of conditions including heavy wet soils in winter and parched dry situations in summer. They are showy as well. What treasures!

Some *Callistemon* plants are low shrubs only about 1 m (40 in) in height, while others are trees 10–15 m (33–50 ft) tall. Many are suitable for screening and hedging purposes. All respond well to pruning, which can encourage bushy growth and increase flower production. A common practice is to cut back behind the flower-spikes immediately after flowering.

Their main flowering period is during spring, when the flower-spikes of cream, green, yellow, pink, mauve or red provide a colourful display. If plants receive moisture and nutrients during summer there will often be a second burst of flower during autumn. Colourful silvery or pink to red new-foliage growth is an added decorative feature of several species.

Callistemon 'Harkness'

The following is a brief selection of the many species and cultivars now available.

Callistemon 'Harkness' (Gawler Hybrid), a large shrub 3–6 m (10–20 ft) tall by a similar width, originated many years ago in South Australia. Its bright red flower-spikes are among the largest, being 15 cm (6 in) or more in length. The branchlets are often slightly pendulous, resulting in an extremely attractive shrub. It grows best in a fairly sunny situation. If your garden is in a region with alkaline soils this *Callistemon* is well worth growing as it is more tolerant of alkalinity than most others.

Callistemon 'Kings Park Special' was introduced to cultivation through the Kings Park Botanic Garden in Perth, Western Australia. It is an excellent cultivar, growing 3–4 m (10–13 ft) tall by a similar width. The main flowering period is during summer when there is a profuse display of brilliant, deep red flowers, usually produced in clusters at the ends of the branchlets.

While most *Callistemon* species have flower-spikes in various shades of red, those of different colours are excellent for variation in the garden. Plants can be grown in close proximity to each other, allowing the branches to intertwine. During the flowering season you can then enjoy delightful combinations of red, yellow, pink and mauve flower-spikes. The white flowers of *Callistemon* 'Anzac' and 'Wilderness White' can be used for added contrast and effect.

Callistemon 'King's Park Special'

Callistemon 'Mauve Mist' is a bushy shrub 2–4 m (6½–13 ft) tall, with soft, silky new-foliage tips. The flower-spikes, seen mainly in spring to summer, are mauve tipped with gold.

Callistemon 'Perth Pink' and *Callistemon* 'Reeves Pink' are two excellent cultivars, each producing pink flower-spikes, mainly in late spring to early summer. Plants grow 2–4 m (6½–13 ft) tall, with 'Perth Pink' being more dense and upright in habit than 'Reeves Pink'.

In addition to their beauty, *Callistemon* flowers are an excellent source of nectar for native honey-eating birds. The bushy growth of the plants also provides shelter and nesting sites for birds.

Bottlebrush flower-spikes can certainly be used as indoor cut-flowers, although they are not grown commercially for this purpose as the flowers easily become crushed during transportation.

There are about 30 species of *Callistemon* native to Australia, and an even greater number of hybrids and cultivars, giving us a wide range to choose from for our gardens.

Callistemon 'Mauve Mist'

Callistemon 'Perth Pink'

Castanospermum australe   BLACK BEAN

This extremely attractive rainforest tree occurs from the Cape York Peninsula, Queensland to north-eastern New South Wales, but will grow and flower well as far south as Melbourne, Victoria.

Plants are generally slow-growing, usually to about 10 m (33 ft) tall, but older trees in their natural habitat can exceed 20 m (66 ft) in height.

The large, divided leaves are deep green with a shiny upper surface. During spring and summer there is a showy display of large pea-flowers, produced in racemes 5–15 cm (2–6 in) long. They are initially greenish yellow then deepen in colour to orange and red as they mature, giving a delightful combination of colours on the tree. In warmer areas the flowers are followed by large woody pods containing three to five chestnut-like seeds.

The seeds are generally regarded as non-edible and poisonous, but it is currently thought that they have medicinal value and this aspect is being investigated in Australia and overseas.

Black Bean timber is highly regarded for wood-turning and cabinet-making but care should be taken to avoid inhalation of fine sawdust while working the wood.

Castanospermum australe

Chamelaucium uncinatum GERALDTON WAX

Geraldton Wax is a very popular cut-flower, with plants being grown for flower markets in Australia and overseas. The waxy, open-petalled, pink, mauve, purplish red or white flowers, 1–2.5 cm (¼–¾ in) across, are produced mainly in spring to early summer.

Chamelaucium uncinatum has short, narrow leaves and is an excellent light screening plant of relatively open habit. Plants need a sunny, well-drained situation for best results. They can grow 2–4 m (6½–13 ft) tall but respond well to pruning or to the picking of the flowering stems; this reduces their size and promotes bushy growth.

Several named selections of Geraldton Wax are available with different flower colours. There are also early and late flowering forms and selections with particularly large flowers. *Chamelaucium uncinatum* 'Album', *Chamelaucium uncinatum* 'Early Pink' and *Chamelaucium uncinatum* 'Purple Pride' are all fairly widely grown.

Selections with a compact growth habit are also now obtainable and these are suitable for smaller gardens or medium to large containers.

Attractive hybrids that have *Chamelaucium uncinatum* as one of the parent plants include *Chamelaucium* 'Meringur Mist' and 'Lady Stephanie', both of which have pale pink flowers in tight heads.

There are over 20 species of *Chamelaucium*, all of which grow naturally in south-western Western Australia.

Chamelaucium uncinatum 'Purple Pride'

Chorizema   FLAME PEAS

There are about 18 *Chorizema* species, all native to Australia. Most produce extremely brightly coloured flowers. They can remain unnoticed in the garden for most of the year, then in late winter to early summer will certainly let you know they are there, as they light up the area with a riot of colour. The pea-flowers are in vivid eye-catching combinations of orange, pinks or reds with yellow.

Most are small shrubs that usually grow less than 1 m (40 in) tall, but if given the opportunity they will often scramble up through other shrubs to a height of 2 m (80 in) or more.

Chorizema varium 'Hybrid' is a popular garden plant that has been grown for many years under the incorrect name of *Chorizema cordatum*. The small, bright green leaves are somewhat heart-shaped, often with a slightly toothed margin. The colourful orange, yellow and purplish pink pea-flowers can be profuse during late winter and spring.

Plants are adaptable to a range of conditions, but usually grow best in

filtered sun or sun for only part of the day, in soils that are moist but well drained. They respond well to pruning after flowering or regular clipping, and are suitable for cultivation in gardens or containers.

For an extremely attractive combination, try growing the Flame Pea with white-flowered plants such as *Eriostemon myoporoides* or *Xanthosia rotundifolia*.

Chorizema varium 'Hybrid'

Chrysocephalum apiculatum 'Golden Buttons'
COMMON EVERLASTING

This is a delightful, low, spreading, sun-loving groundcover plant with green to grey–green leaves and tight heads of small, golden, everlasting flowers produced on short upright stems almost throughout the year. Botanically it is part of a complex group of plants sold over the years under several different names. For many years it was known as *Helichrysum apiculatum* 'Golden Buttons' or *Helichrysum ramosissimum* 'Tall Form' and has also been available under the wrong name of *Helichrysum amplexans*.

Common Everlasting will grow well in most soils, from sands to heavy clay loams, provided there is relatively good drainage.

The main flowering period begins about mid-spring and continues to late autumn. As some of the spent flowers become brownish in mid-summer it is good to give plants a relatively hard pruning. Plants can be sheared back to near ground level as new growth begins to appear at the base of the older stems. This tidies them up and encourages new foliage, which should develop relatively quickly. There will be scattered flowers during winter, then as spring approaches you will notice another burst of new foliage, together with the buds for the coming season.

Chrysocephalum apiculatum 'Golden Buttons', foreground

Although this plant suckers lightly, it is modest in its travels and could never be described as rampant. If it does venture slightly further than you would wish, simply dig up the offending suckers and transplant them elsewhere in the garden, or put them in a pot ready to give to friends or your next fundraising stall.

The golden, papery, everlasting flower-heads are about 1.5 cm (½ in) across and are produced in clusters at the ends of the stalks. They are excellent for making small posies or for other small-scale floral-art or craft purposes.

There are several other forms of this species. Some selections have green foliage, while short silky hairs on the stems and leaves can give other forms a grey or even silvery appearance.

Chrysocephalum apiculatum

Correa CORREAS

Correas have no common name apart from their botanical name, which undoubtedly is a fairly easy name to remember anyway.

There are 11 species, all of which are native to Australia, but we can obtain 50 or more different correas from nurseries if we include the numerous forms and hybrids now being grown.

There are several low, spreading groundcovers, numerous small to medium shrubs, and one species that can grow to a small tree of 6 m (20 ft) or more in height. All respond well to pruning, which encourages bushy growth. Most correas grow best in filtered sun or sun for part of the day only, and will flower happily in sun or shade, so they are very useful plants in the garden. They can certainly light up a dull corner on a winter's day.

The main flowering period of the correas is through autumn, winter and early spring, but some flower happily in late spring and summer. The flowers are usually tubular and hang like small bells on the bushes. The most common colours are green, pink, or red tipped with green. Some flowers are in shades of cream, yellow and orange, with several combining two or more colours.

Nectar-feeding birds find correa flowers extremely attractive, particularly as they provide an excellent source of food during the winter months.

Correa pulchella (Beautiful Correa) is a variable species with very brightly coloured bells, in colours that include pinks, orange–reds, reds and occasionally clear white. Plants are usually small shrubs about 1 m (40 in) tall, but some selections are prostrate groundcovers.

This species will grow well in full sun or sun for just part of the day. Beautiful Correa will be happy in most soils, including those that are alkaline, as long as they are well drained.

Correa pulchella

Correa reflexa (Common Correa) is an extremely variable species. In this group of plants there are forms with flower-bells of cream, green, yellow, pinks and reds, or a variety of combinations of these colours. The bells can be long and narrow, long and broad or short and squat, while the plants vary from being low, spreading groundcovers to shrubs 1–2 m (40–80 in) tall. There are numerous selections of this species available through nurseries, and an even wider range of hybrids with *Correa reflexa* as one parent.

Correa reflexa

Corymbia CORYMBIAS

Corymbia is a recently named genus of Australian plants consisting of 113 species. Eighty of these were previously included in *Eucalyptus* and 33 are newly named species. For further information on closely related trees, see *Eucalyptus*, page 78.

In general *Corymbia* contains those former species of *Eucalyptus* commonly known as Bloodwoods, and also takes in the Ghost Gum group.

Many are trees not commonly grown in gardens, but two in particular are very popular in cultivation.

Corymbia citriodora (Lemon-scented Gum; formerly *Eucalyptus citriodora*) is a truly majestic tree with a magnificent smooth white trunk that can grow to 25 m (82 ft) or more in height, so it should be considered for large areas only. The leaves have a delightful lemon–eucalyptus fragrance and the foliage is used for commercial distilling of the oil. Clusters of small white flowers are produced in late winter to spring.

The Lemon-scented Gum occurs naturally in Queensland. It will grow in most well-drained soils and although frost-tender when young it acquires greater resistance as the tree matures.

Corymbia ficifolia (Red-flowering Gum; formerly *Eucalyptus ficifolia*) is a native of Western Australia. It produces one of the most stunning displays of all flowering trees, with blooms that can range in colour from creamy white through various shades of pink to red, orange–red or deep red. It is not possible to guarantee the flower colour of

Corymbia citriodora

plants produced from seed, but colour-guaranteed grafted plants are now obtainable. The shades most commonly selected for grafting are bright red and orange. Flowering is mainly during summer and early autumn.

The Red-flowering Gum grows best in a warm, well-drained situation where it can reach 10–15 m (33–50 ft) tall. Grafted plants generally develop as smaller, more compact trees and they usually flower when they are much younger than trees grown from seedlings.

Corymbia ficifolia

Crinum pedunculatum   SWAMP LILY

It is not uncommon for white flowers to have delightfully enjoyable fragrances and this Australian lily is certainly one plant that comes into this category. The fragrance is there to encourage pollinating insects to visit the flowers, but we can enjoy the perfume also, especially in late afternoon and the evening, through an open window or as we walk in the garden.

There are over 100 *Crinum* species throughout the world, with about ten per cent occurring in Australia. Some species are widely cultivated, while others are not well known.

Crinum pedunculatum is from coastal and near-coastal regions of eastern Queensland and New South Wales. It is often found beside waterways or in areas of poor drainage but also grows successfully in well-drained situations. Plants will happily tolerate full open sunshine or partial sun.

The Swamp Lily is becoming increasingly popular in cultivation, forming large tussocks or clumps with leaves to over 1 m (40 in) long,

arising from the bulbous root system. Broad, loose clusters of attractive white flowers, each up to 10 cm (4 in) across, are produced on upright stems during spring to late summer.

Crinum pedunculatum has a bold growth habit and provides an attractive and dramatic impact when plants are grown among small shrubs or other clump-forming species.

Crinum pedunculatum

Crowea saligna WILLOW-LEAVED CROWEA

This showy small shrub grows to 1.5 m (5 ft) tall by a similar width, but plants respond well to pruning and can easily be kept about 1 m (40 in) high, or restricted to a narrower width.

Croweas are excellent small shrubs for the provision of autumn colour in the garden. They start flowering in mid-summer and can continue into early winter. There are three species in this plant group, all native to Australia, and usually with pale to deep pink flowers. A small number of named cultivars are also now becoming popular for garden use, including some prostrate forms and an unusual white-flowered crowea that is sometimes available in nurseries.

Crowea saligna has the largest flowers of the genus, with the starry pink blooms being about 3.5 cm (1¼ in) in diameter. Plants occur naturally in the Sydney sandstone area of New South Wales. They like relatively well-drained soils and a situation with filtered sun or sun for part of the day.

The flowering stems can be picked for use indoors and are quite long-lasting as cut-flowers. *Crowea saligna* and some forms of *Crowea exalata* are both grown commercially for this purpose. *Crowea exalata* has smaller flowers and the leaves have a lovely aniseed fragrance.

Crowea saligna

59

Dampiera   DAMPIERAS

Dampieras are named after the English explorer, navigator and buccaneer William Dampier, who sailed to Australia in the eighteenth century and collected plants from Western Australia.

There are over 60 species of *Dampiera*, and most have eye-catching blue flowers ranging from soft pale to rich deep blues or vivid bluish purples. They are extremely colourful and include some of the world's finest blue-flowered plants.

Most dampieras are low, perennial herbs. Many are excellent for garden cultivation and some will spread by suckering lightly if conditions are favourable.

Dampiera diversifolia is a densely foliaged, low, mat-forming species from Western Australia. The flowers are usually rich blue and provide a showy display, mainly during spring. Its favourite location is in partial or filtered sun, with moist but well-drained soils. This is also an excellent plant for growing in containers or hanging baskets and can be grown as a groundcover in combination with other taller plants in medium to large containers.

Dampiera linearis (Common Dampiera) is a variable species with several different selections available. Most have rich blue flowers, often with a touch of white or yellow in the centre. The foliage can be green or covered with tiny whitish hairs to give a greyish appearance. The flowering times of the different selections can vary considerably, with some providing scattered flowers throughout the year, and others having a dense, rich display, seen mainly during spring (see illustration opposite).

Dampiera rosmarinifolia (Rosemary Dampiera) is not as dense and compact as the two species described above but will sucker informally

Dampiera diversifolia

Dampiera stricta 'Glasshouse Glory'

through a garden bed, providing blue, purple, mauve–pink or almost white flowers during spring to early summer. The leaves are similar in appearance to those of the well-known herb Rosemary but without the same fragrance (see frontispiece).

Dampiera stricta 'Glasshouse Glory' is a long-flowering and very showy plant, with bright mid-blue flowers produced throughout most of the year. It grows well in partial or full sun, in soils that are well-drained but not excessively dry. Plants sucker lightly and, if you wish, some of the suckers can be dug up and re-established in pots for planting out elsewhere in the garden. This dampiera is also excellent for containers and medium to large hanging baskets.

A garden with eye-catching plants of *Dampiera linearis*

Darwinia DARWINIAS

Darwinia is another group of Australian plants in which the genus name is also the most frequently used common name, although plants from around the Stirling Ranges region of Western Australia are often known also as Bells, for example Fringed Bell, Mountain Bell and Stirling Bell. There are over 30 species occurring in Western Australia, ten in New South Wales, and between two and four in Queensland, South Australia and Victoria. They were named not after the famous naturalist Charles Darwin, but after his grandfather, Erasmus Darwin (1731–1802).

Darwinia citriodora (Lemon-scented Darwinia) is one of the most commonly grown and adaptable of the genus. It has somewhat small, bluish green, oval to heart-shaped leaves with a spicy rather than a strongly lemon-scented fragrance, despite the fact that *citriodora* means 'lemon-scented'. Plants usually grow 1–1.5 m (40–60 in) tall but smaller-growing, ground-hugging selections are also obtainable. Clusters of small orange–red and green flowers are produced over a long period, with the peak flowering in winter and spring.

This *Darwinia* is adaptable to a wide range of soil and climatic conditions and is widely used as the rootstock for grafting some of the less tolerant species. It usually grows best in partial or filtered sun, with slightly moist but well-drained soils. The taller forms are excellent for low hedging.

Darwinia lejostyla (Stirling Bell) is one of several Western Australian species in which the flower clusters are surrounded by larger bracts to

Darwinia citriodora

produce a showy bell-like flower-head. Plants grow 0.5–1 m (20–40 in) tall and have small, narrow leaves. During spring to early summer there is an eye-catching display of reddish pink and white flower-heads. This darwinia likes to have well-drained soils or sands. It prefers an open situation rather than being crowded among other plants and will grow in partial or full sun. It is frequently cultivated on its own roots but is also usually available as a grafted plant, in which *Darwinia citriodora* rootstock has been used for greater adaptability and reliability.

Other darwinias with showy bell-shaped flower-heads similar to those of *Darwinia lejostyla* and with similar requirements in cultivation include *Darwinia meeboldii* (Cranbrook Bell) and *Darwinia oxylepis* (Gilham's Bell).

Darwinia lejostyla

Dendrobium ORCHIDS

Dendrobium orchids occur from Asia to Australia. There are about 1500 species, most of which are epiphytes, growing naturally on the trunks or branches of trees or shrubs. Some grow on rocks or in rock crevices. Dendrobiums are not parasites and do not draw nourishment from host plants, but use them primarily for support and the provision of a suitable growing environment. Epiphytic plants also gain moisture from the droplets of rain that run down the trunk of the host plant and to the orchid's root area.

Epiphytic orchids can be cultivated in a way that imitates their natural habitat by attaching them to slabs of timber or other similar supports, or to selected tree trunks. Most will also grow well in containers of a freely draining orchid potting mixture. Some will grow well in rockeries, but a well-drained site is essential.

Dendrobium kingianum (Pink Rock Orchid) is the most widely grown and easily cultivated of the Australian dendrobiums. It grows naturally on rocks and boulders or in crevices on rocky cliff faces and is a clump-forming orchid about 50 cm (20 in) tall. Sprays of up to 15 pale pink, pink, mauve–pink or reddish flowers are produced during spring. Plants grow very successfully in pots or hanging baskets, with best results in airy but humid situations. Several named selections of the Pink Rock Orchid are obtainable, as well as numerous hybrids with this orchid as one of the parent species.

Dendrobium kingianum

There is nothing modest about the flower-spikes of *Dendrobium speciosum* (Rock Orchid or King Orchid). They can be 60 cm (2 ft) long, bearing sometimes over a hundred fragrant, white, cream or yellow flowers, each up to 5 cm (2 in) across. The flowering period is late winter to spring.

This is a large clump-forming orchid, with thick, leathery leaves up to 25 cm (10 in) long. Plants grow slowly to forms clumps over 2 m (80 in) across. In cultivation they can if you wish be divided into several smaller clumps before reaching this size.

Dendrobium speciosum can be grown in a container of coarse, well-drained potting mixture or attached to a solid wooden slab or old tree trunk. It will also grow well in garden situations such as well-drained rock crevices.

In nature this orchid is found from north-eastern Queensland to eastern Victoria. It grows best in situations with filtered sunlight or sun for most of the day. Plants tend to flower best in warm climates, so they should be planted in a warm position and sheltered from cold winds in southern Australia.

Dendrobium speciosum

Dicksonia antarctica   SOFT TREE-FERN

This popular fern occurs in moist, cool forest gullies in eastern Australia, from Queensland to Tasmania. It has large, glossy dark green fronds, 2–4 m (6½–13 ft) long, that radiate from the central fibrous trunk. Young plants develop quite quickly into low, spreading plants, but the fibrous trunk takes many years to reach its full height, which can exceed 10 m (33 ft).

This particular tree-fern can be readily transplanted by sawing off the trunk near ground level, removing most of the fronds to reduce the plant's moisture requirements, then relocating it in the desired position. The Soft Tree-fern is commonly sold in this way by nurseries but it should be pointed out that this method of relocation is not appropriate for most other tree-fern species.

Dicksonia antarctica is often thought to be the Female Tree-fern, with *Cyathea australis*, the Rough or Hard Tree-fern, being described as the Male Tree-fern. This is not correct.

Ferns are non-flowering plants that reproduce through the production of

spores, contained in brown or blackish spore-cases on the undersides of the fronds. Young sporelings of *Dicksonia antarctica* will sometimes develop in the garden if conditions are suitable, or the spore can be collected for propagation under more favourable conditions. Some patience is needed, however, in regard to the propagation and initial cultivation of all fern species.

The Soft Tree-fern likes cool, moist soils and prefers shade, partial shade or filtered sun. Plants will grow well in gardens or large containers and transplanted specimens can be excellent for providing quick, tall growth in sheltered situations.

Dicksonia antarctica

Diplarrena moraea BUTTERFLY FLAG

The Butterfly Flag is a member of the iris family. The common name refers to the attractive white flowers that are produced on slender upright stems during spring to early summer and resemble butterflies fluttering in the breeze.

There are two species of *Diplarrena*, both native to Australia, with this one occurring in New South Wales, Victoria and Tasmania. The other, *Diplarrena latifolia*, is found only in Tasmania.

The Butterfly Flag is an adaptable species in cultivation, growing in full sun, partial sun or filtered sun and in moisture-retentive acidic soils that have moderately good drainage. Plants are frost-tolerant.

They form clumps of evergreen foliage to about 60 cm (2 ft) tall with narrow strap-like green leaves. During spring to early summer erect flower-stems bear a delightful display of mainly white flowers with yellow and purple central colouration and a pleasing honey-like fragrance. The flowers are short-lived but are produced over an extended period.

Diplarrena moraea is excellent for providing erect, clumping growth in a garden to contrast with other shrubby plants, adding a feature often sadly missed when plants of this form are omitted from garden designs. If you have a spot in the garden where you feel something is needed to add variety, try including a grassy plant or an iris relative such as this Butterfly Flag: it may be just what you want!

Diplarrena moraea

Doodia aspera PRICKLY RASP FERN

The Prickly Rasp Fern is an excellent garden plant. We nearly always think of ferns as being green plants, with little or no other colour provided by the foliage, and there are of course no flowers to give additional colour. One glance at this *Doodia* tells us that this is no ordinary green fern. The new young fronds can vary from being slightly reddish to spectacular, with coppery to bright red tonings even more brilliant when backlit by sunshine.

We also sometimes think of ferns as growing only in moist, heavily shaded situations. There are, however, several species that will grow well in partial or even full sun and the Prickly Rasp Fern is one of these. It is a fern that likes moisture-retentive, acidic soils that are fairly well-drained. The plant does not enjoy extended periods of waterlogging.

The Prickly Rasp Fern grows from a creeping underground rootstock and forms small, dense colonies of plants, with upright fronds to a height of 20–40 cm (8–16 in). It is found naturally in Queensland, New South Wales and Victoria.

Doodia aspera will do well in a wide range of garden situations and can also be grown successfully in containers and hanging baskets. It is certainly a fern with a difference—and an attractive one at that! The closely allied *Doodia caudata* and *Doodia media* have similar qualities.

Doodia aspera

Doryanthes excelsa   GYMEA LILY, FLAME LILY, ILLAWARRA LILY

There is certainly a dramatic presence associated with this majestic Australian plant. It is a clump-forming species with leaves about 1.5 m (5 ft) long, forming a clump 1.5 m (5 ft) tall by 2–3 m (6½–10 ft) across. During spring and summer, large dark red flowers are produced in globular heads about 30 cm (12 in) across, on thick upright stems, sometimes exceeding 3 m (10 ft) in height. It can be exciting to watch the flower-stems developing on garden plants, as they take many months to reach full flowering maturity.

Doryanthes excelsa occurs naturally in the sandstone areas around Sydney, New South Wales. It likes well-drained soils with some organic, moisture-retaining content and a situation that receives partial to full sun or filtered sunlight.

Plants can be slow to flower initially and do not always flower every year in a garden, but they are perennial. They do not die after flowering like the introduced Century Plant, *Agave americana*, which is also a clump-forming plant with very tall flower-stems.

There are two species in the genus *Doryanthes*. The other, *Doryanthes palmeri* (Spear Lily) occurs in south-eastern Queensland and New South Wales, and differs in that the red flowers extend for up to 1 m (40 in) along the thick flower-stem (see illustration on page 8). This species grows well in similar conditions to *Doryanthes excelsa*.

Left and below: *Doryanthes excelsa*

Dryandra formosa SHOWY DRYANDRA

Showy Dryandra is a very appropriate common name for this plant, which has breathtakingly beautiful flower-heads. The central portion of the flower has a lovely 'touch-me' silky texture just before the flower becomes fully mature. Flowering is mainly during spring and the flower-heads, up to 10 cm (4 in) across, have a delightful combination of yellow–orange with burnt-orange bracts. They are popular as long-lasting cut-flowers and continue to be decorative when dried.

Dryandra formosa grows as a shrub of 3 m (10 ft) or more in height with stiff, toothed (but not prickly) green leaves up to 20 cm (8 in) long. It occurs naturally in south-western Western Australia and for good results in cultivation must have sandy soils or well-drained loams with partial or full sun. Plants require little or no fertiliser and can react adversely to phosphorus-rich fertilisers. Once established they usually grow best without supplementary watering during dry periods.

There are over 50 species of *Dryandra*, all native to south-western Western Australia. They are members of the Proteaceae family.

Dryandra formosa

Elaeocarpus reticulatus   BLUEBERRY ASH

If you are wanting an attractive, small to medium tree for the garden, the Blueberry Ash could be just the species you are looking for.

Elaeocarpus reticulatus occurs along the east coast of Australia and is adaptable to a fairly wide range of conditions. Plants usually grow 6–10 m (20–33 ft) tall in cultivation. They have dark green, glossy, somewhat oblong leaves, up to 10 cm (4 in) long, that attain bright red tonings before they are shed sporadically throughout the year.

During spring to summer there is a delightful display of delicate, fringed, bell-shaped flowers, appearing somewhat like 'fairies' petticoats'. Selections with white, pale pink or deep pink flowers are all now fairly readily obtainable.

As the flowers mature they are replaced by small, globular, shiny, dark blue, somewhat olive-like fruits, providing an added attraction from late autumn to early spring. The fruits are eaten by birds and although seedlings can sometimes result, the seed is regarded as being fairly difficult to germinate.

The Blueberry Ash will grow in a wide range of garden conditions, preferring organically rich, well-drained soils. It does well in both shady and sunny positions.

Elaeocarpus reticulatus

Epacris HEATHS

There are just under 50 species of *Epacris*, occurring mainly in eastern Australia but found also in New Zealand and New Caledonia. They are in some ways similar to the heathers or ericas, which do not occur in the Australasian region, and the two groups are frequently confused.

Many species of *Epacris* are very showy when in flower, bearing masses of small tubular flowers that can be white or in various shades of pink through to deep red. Some include combinations of these colours.

Epacris impressa (Common Heath) grows naturally in New South Wales, Victoria, Tasmania and South Australia and is adaptable to a wide range of well-drained soils. It is usually a fairly upright plant 0.5–1.5 m (1½–5 ft) tall, with short, slightly prickly leaves; but plants will be bushier if pruned regularly, during or immediately after flowering. This also helps to maintain good health and vigour. Flowering is mainly during autumn and winter, with a colourful display of tubular flowers from white through to bright red. They are rich in nectar and eagerly visited by small honey-eating birds.

The Common Heath is not readily noticed in the garden when not in bloom. It blends with other more dominant foliages and is best grown in the company of other plants. This *Epacris* was extremely popular in England during the early nineteenth century and numerous named selections were grown. Today a limited number of forms are available from nurseries, providing some very colourful garden plants.

Epacris longiflora (Fuchsia Heath) is from New South Wales and southern Queensland and is an extremely showy plant. Pendent tubular flowers are produced almost

Epacris impressa

throughout the year, although peak flowering is usually in winter and summer. The elongated bells are usually bright red tipped with white, but selections with pink or all-white flowers are also obtainable.

Fuchsia Heath likes well-drained soils and prefers a situation with partial or filtered sunshine. It grows well in gardens and is also excellent for containers or hanging baskets. If plants are left without pruning, the flower-bells can extend for 30 cm (12 in) or more along the arching branchlets, while light pruning will encourage bushier growth and numerous, smaller clusters of flowers.

Epacris longiflora

Eremophila EMU BUSHES

The name *Eremophila* means a lover of desert, desolate or lonely places, and this can certainly describe the habitat of many of the plants in this Australian genus. They occur in all mainland states of Australia, with the majority being native to the inland, arid regions. The common name Emu Bush results from the seeds and fruits being a popular food for native emus.

There are over 200 *Eremophila* species and cultivars and many are very attractive and desirable garden plants. A small number are adaptable to a range of garden situations, but those from dry areas must have excellent drainage in an open sunny situation. Some respond poorly to humid and overcast weather and will only do well where these conditions do not occur.

Eremophila maculata (Spotted Emu Bush or Spotted Fuchsia) is a variable and very adaptable species. Plants like a sunny position and will grow in most well-drained soils. Several different forms are available, with flower colours including yellow or orange, pale to deep pink, and red or purplish red. The common names refer to the flowers usually having spotted throats.

Some forms of *Eremophila maculata* are low and spreading while others can grow to 2 m (6½ ft) or more in height. The red-flowered selection illustrated here is a shrubby plant 1–2 m (40–80 in) tall by a similar width. Plants respond well to pruning or to the picking of the flowers; this results in an attractive, dense, bushy habit. The flowering period is mainly during winter and spring.

Most readers are not likely to be able to encourage emus to the garden by planting eremophilas, but the flowers of this selection will certainly encourage the smaller nectar-feeding birds.

Eremophila nivea (Silver

Eremophila maculata

Emu Bush) is a most spectacular plant for gardens or containers. It flowers from late winter through to early summer and sporadically at other times, when its tubular lilac flowers contrast delightfully with the silvery grey foliage.

This *Eremophila* is native to Western Australia, where it grows in well-drained soils in open sunny situations. In cultivation it likes similar conditions for best results. For increased tolerance in cultivation grafted plants are now available, but it is still important that it should be grown in a sunny, open position where it is not overcrowded. In species such as this, where the soft foliage is covered by many small fine hairs, air movement is important to prevent the leaves from remaining wet for extended periods. Without adequate air movement the conditions become ideal for the spread of fungal diseases.

Eremophila nivea can grow to 2 m (80 in) tall by a similar width. Plants respond well to a light or moderate pruning, which can be commenced from a very early age, and they can be easily maintained at a smaller size if desired. The cutting of flowering stems is an excellent form of pruning, as they remain attractive indoors for a considerable time.

Eremophila nivea

Eriostemon WAX FLOWERS

The *Eriostemon* species are members of the citrus family, Rutaceae, although their fruits look nothing at all like oranges or lemons. There are over 30 species, all occurring only in Australia. Several are excellent garden plants and some are also grown commercially for cut-flower production.

Eriostemon myoporoides (Long-leaf Wax Flower) is the most commonly cultivated and certainly deserves its popularity. Several forms are available, including attractive shrubby selections 1.5–2 m (5–6½ ft) tall by a similar width. The dark green leaves have numerous oil glands and are distinctively aromatic. During winter to spring clusters of pink buds open to reveal a profuse display of five-petalled, starry, white, lightly fragrant flowers. They provide an extremely showy display in the garden, or can be cut and used for indoor decoration.

Long-leaf Wax Flower is extremely adaptable in cultivation. It has a preference for fairly well-drained soils and while it likes filtered or partial

Eriostemon myoporoides

sun it will also grow and flower well in full sun. It is hardy to moderate frosts and extended dry periods once established. Plants respond extremely well to pruning, which promotes bushy and vigorous growth.

Eriostemon verrucosus is a variable species and one very attractive low shrub is the selection known as *Eriostemon verrucosus* 'Semmens Double Wax Flower'. It is 30–60 cm (1–2 ft) tall by 50 cm–1 m (20–40 in) across, with aromatic, slightly warty foliage. Pink buds and small multi-petalled white flowers, appearing like miniature white waterlilies, are produced in late winter to spring.

This *Eriostemon* likes a sunny or semi-shaded situation with well-drained soils. Plants are suitable for gardens or are excellent for cultivation in containers and hanging baskets. They can sometimes sucker lightly, which is a desirable feature in most situations. Plants respond well to pruning. This can be used to encourage denser growth or to restrict their size if necessary.

Eriostemon verrucosus 'Semmens Double Wax Flower'

Eucalyptus EUCALYPTS

Eucalyptus is the most significant genus of Australian plants. Eucalypts have a range of common names and the one by which they are best known is Gum Tree, even though this names relates correctly to some but not all of the species.

Recent research has resulted in the formation of the new genus of *Corymbia,* to which 80 former species of *Eucalyptus* have now been transferred, along with 33 newly described species. Over 500 species remain in the *Eucalyptus* genus, which means it is still a very large group of Australian plants.

Many eucalypts grow much too large for the average garden, although they are certainly worthy of a place in broad-scale private and public landscaping projects. Some are grown primarily for their habit and for their provision of shade and shelter, and some have aromatic foliage, attractive trunks, showy flowers or decorative and dramatic buds and fruits. There are of course also other uses for these trees, including the production of timber and as honey-flora plants highly prized by apiarists. Eucalyptus oil is obtained from the foliage and is valuable for medicinal, cleaning and other purposes, while many of the species with blue–green leaves are widely used as cut-foliage in floristry.

With such a large number of species, and a distribution that extends throughout Australia, it is not possible to generalise in regard to growing conditions. Some like dry soils; others are known as swamp gums because they tolerate wet soil; many tolerate shade; the snow gums are tolerant of extreme cold; and others are ideal for coastal planting. Here we have selected four species of *Eucalyptus* (and see also two species of *Corymbia,* page 54) to give a representative covering of these trees and perhaps to

Eucalyptus caesia subspecies *magna* 'Silver Princess'

encourage you to check out the full range of these two groups whenever you need an evergreen small to tall tree.

Eucalyptus caesia subspecies *magna* 'Silver Princess' is a stunningly beautiful tree, usually growing 6–8 m (20–26 ft) tall, with reddish brown curling bark on the trunk. The long, narrow leaves are grey–green and the weeping reddish branchlets have a whitish bloom that gives them the appearance of being dusted with white powder. During winter and spring, silver-dusted buds open to reveal large pink flowers tipped with gold.

'Silver Princess' needs a sunny, open, well-drained situation. Young plants can grow quickly and become loose in the ground, so heavy fertilising and watering is not recommended in the initial years. Pruning can help to promote sturdier growth and the removal of heavy clusters of gumnuts after flowering can reduce the weight on the branches.

Eucalyptus citriodora (Lemon-scented Gum)—now *Corymbia citriodora*, page 56.

Eucalyptus ficifolia (Red-flowering Gum)—now *Corymbia ficifolia*, page 56.

Eucalyptus forrestiana (Fuchsia Gum) is another of the relatively small and highly attractive eucalypts from Western Australia. It is an unusual species as it is grown for its colourful buds and fruits rather than for its decorative flowers. It is a small tree, only 3–7 m (10–23 ft) tall, and flowers mainly through summer and autumn. The flowers are yellow, while the pendent buds and fruits can be a vivid orange–red. They are retained on the tree for a long period and are of excellent ornamental value.

The Fuchsia Gum needs a warm, sunny situation. It likes well-drained soils but appreciates some moist to wet periods during winter. Plants are tolerant of both drought and frosts once well established.

Eucalyptus leucoxylon is a variable species, known in different areas by the common names of White Ironbark, Yellow Gum and Blue Gum. While the species includes large white-flowered trees about 30 m (99 ft) tall, there are also some much smaller selections about 10 m (33 ft) tall, with cream, pink or sometimes yellow flowers, and these are very popular for garden use.

These dwarf forms of *Eucalyptus leucoxylon* have attractive trunks, with smooth creamy white to grey bark that is deciduous in late summer and autumn. The selections most popularly available are those with pink flowers, although flower colour is variable and cannot be guaranteed in plants grown from seed. This is an adaptable tree in cultivation and will grow in a wide range of well-drained soils. It is tolerant of frost and drought and all forms are highly bird-attracting when in flower.

Eucalyptus preissiana (Bell-fruited Mallee) grows as a large, spreading shrub rather than a tree. Plants can grow 2–5 m (6½–16½ ft) tall by a

Eucalyptus leucoxylon, dwarf form

similar width, with smooth grey bark and thick, greyish green leaves. Its showy flowers make it certainly worthy of cultivation. The vivid yellow flowers produced during winter and spring can be 5 cm (2 in) across and are followed by broad, bell-shaped woody gumnuts.

This Western Australian eucalypt prefers a warm to hot, well-drained situation. Plants respond well to pruning and flowering branches are excellent for long-lasting indoor use.

Eucalyptus preissiana

Grevillea SPIDER FLOWERS

There are over 250 species of *Grevillea* and almost as many additional cultivars and hybrids, many of which are popular garden plants. They vary from being prostrate groundcovers to the large Silky Oak (*Grevillea robusta*). There is wide variation in foliage shapes and the flowers include a huge range of colours. All species occur within Australia except five that are native to Papua New Guinea, New Caledonia and Indonesia.

Many grevilleas are excellent garden plants. Some flower throughout the year and most are extremely attractive to nectar-feeding birds.

Grevillea dimorpha, narrow-leaf form

A selection of some of the most popular grevilleas is included, but of course there are many others to choose from for garden planting. Most nurseries, particularly those specialising in Australian plants, can help in this regard.

The Flame Grevillea (*Grevillea dimorpha*) is a very showy shrub with bright red flowers in autumn, winter and spring. The deep green leaves can be narrow, as the illustration shows, or up to 3 cm (1 in) wide. They are commonly known as broad-leaf or narrow-leaf forms. The narrow-leaf forms usually grow to less than 1 m (40 in) tall, while those with broader leaves can reach 2 m (6½ ft) or more in height. All respond well to pruning.

Grevillea dimorpha occurs in the Grampians region of Victoria. Plants are adaptable to a wide range of garden conditions, provided there is good drainage.

These plants were at one stage included as forms of *Grevillea speciosa*, and you may find them available from nurseries as *Grevillea speciosa* subspecies *dimorpha*.

Grevillea lanigera

The prostrate forms of *Grevillea lanigera* (Woolly Grevillea) are well worth considering if you are looking for a dense groundcover with greyish green leaves and reddish pink and cream flowers through winter and spring. They grow best in well-drained, sunny or semi-shaded situations and are even able to tolerate harsh coastal exposure. Plants respond well to pruning but if left unchecked can grow about 40 cm (16 in) tall by 1–2 m (40–80 in) across.

Grevillea lavandulacea (Lavender Grevillea) has been given its name because the greyish leaves are somewhat similar in appearance to those of Lavender although they do not have the same fragrance. The flowers are bright pink to red, making a delightful contrast to the greyish foliage. They are produced mainly in winter to spring, with sometimes a further flowering in late summer. Several named selections are available, varying in size from small to medium shrubs. In nature they are found in warm, well-drained regions of Victoria and South Australia. All forms respond well to pruning, which can help to maintain healthy, compact growth. They are excellent for gardens or containers.

Grevillea 'Moonlight' is a large shrub that can exceed 3 m (10 ft) in height, so you need ample room for plants such as this in the garden. The leaves are about 20 cm (8 in) long and divided into narrow segments that are dark green on the upper surface and pale silvery green below. Long cream flower-spikes are produced almost throughout the year, making this an excellent shrub for beauty in the garden and also as a nectar source for native birds. Plants grow best in a sunny or semi-shaded site, and need well-drained soils.

Grevillea lavandulacea

Grevillea 'Moonlight'

We have *Grevillea* 'Moonlight' planted very close to *Grevillea* 'Sylvia', which is of similar size and foliage but with reddish pink flower-spikes. The branches of the two shrubs intertwine quite happily and the result is a delightful combination of reddish pink and cream flowers throughout most of the year. Two plants occupy almost no more space than one would, and when they are positioned very close to each other it often means that the plants do not grow as large as they might without such competition.

The flowers of *Grevillea* 'Moonlight' and other similar cultivars are very attractive for indoor use, and the cutting of flowering stems will help promote bushy growth and additional flower production.

Grevillea 'Pink Surprise' is a magnificent large shrub that can grow 3–5 m (10–16½ ft) tall and flower almost throughout the year. The leaves are dark green above and silvery underneath, with deep lobes extending almost to the midrib. The erect flower-spikes, up to 15 cm (6 in) long, are a rich pink with creamy white. Plants need well-drained soils and like a warm situation to stimulate flower production.

The flowers of 'Pink Surprise' are rich in nectar

Grevillea 'Pink Surprise'

and the long flowering period means that an almost constant source of food is available for native honey-eating birds, which add their own beauty and fascination in the garden.

Grevillea robusta (Silky Oak), a large tree from the rainforests of south-eastern Queensland and north-eastern New South Wales, is popular in cultivation throughout many different areas of the world, including Asia, Europe and North America.

The trunk has grey, deeply furrowed bark and the large, ferny leaves are dark green above and greyish underneath. During spring to early summer the trees can become almost dazzling with their brilliant display of bright orange–yellow flowers.

The Silky Oak is adaptable to a wide range of well-drained situations but as the trees can grow to 25 m (82 ft) or more in height they are not ideally suited to small gardens. They will tolerate pruning, but harsh

Grevillea robusta

cutting often destroys their natural beauty. Young plants are suitable for use as indoor container plants.

Silky Oak timber is highly prized for woodworking and furniture-making.

Grevillea 'Robyn Gordon' has become an extremely popular garden plant since its introduction in 1975. It grows about 1.5 m (5 ft) tall and has stiff, divided leaves. Deep pink-red to rose-red flowers are produced in racemes up to 13 cm (5 in) long, almost throughout the year. It is an excellent bird-attracting plant.

This showy cultivar likes full or partial sun and a position with moist but well-drained soils. Plants respond well to regular light or moderate pruning, which should be done at least once a year.

Grevillea 'Superb'

Grevillea 'Superb' is similar in growth habit and foliage to *Grevillea* 'Robyn Gordon' but the large, semi-pendent flower racemes combine yellow, pink and deep pinkish red to give an overall apricot colouring. Here again is a most attractive shrubby *Grevillea* that can flower throughout the year. It provides a delightful alternative for those who wish to avoid bright red flowers.

Grevillea 'Superb' likes a sunny situation with relatively well-drained soils. It is recommended that plants be pruned each year.

Most of the groundcover and shrubby grevilleas respond very well to regular light pruning, and this can be commenced from a very early age to ensure the development of attractive, bushy plants. There are several species that can be grown as standards or regularly clipped for hedging.

Grevilleas generally prefer well-drained soils and many are drought-tolerant once well established in the garden. Their nutritional requirements are not high and they particularly dislike any excessive use of phosphorus-rich fertilisers. A light application of a low-phosphorus, slow-release fertiliser in early spring is usually all that is needed to maintain good healthy growth.

Hakea   HAKEAS

There are about 150 species of *Hakea,* all of which are native to Australia. They are closely related to grevilleas, but usually have two-seeded woody fruits that may be retained on the plants for several years.

Hakea francisiana (Narukalja) is a very showy species from South Australia and Western Australia. Plants can grow with a shrubby habit and to a height of 3–4 m (10–13 ft), or as a small tree to almost double this height. The silvery green leaves have a pointed but not sharp tip. From late winter to early summer the deep pink to reddish flowers are arranged in spikes to 10 cm (4 in) long and provide an eye-catching display.

If plants are pruned from an early stage this will encourage low bushy growth; otherwise you will need to look upwards to see the flowers, which are produced mainly near the top of the plant.

Narukalja grows best in a warm, sunny situation, in sandy or other very well drained soils. To enable plants to be grown with greater success in heavier soil types this species is often sold as a grafted plant using *Hakea salicifolia* as the rootstock.

Hakea laurina (Pincushion Hakea) is one of the best known of all the hakeas. It has been cultivated for many years and its attractive, globular flower clusters have ensured its popularity in gardens both in Australia and overseas.

An important reason for choosing this particular hakea is that its main flowering time is during autumn and winter, when we are often looking for some extra colour in the garden.

The flower-balls are about 7 cm (2¾ in) across and are deep pink to red

with cream styles, giving the appearance of pins in a pincushion, as suggested by the common name. Sometimes as the flowers age the styles also take on a reddish tone, providing a combination of flower colours on the one plant. Often the plants have lovely bronze new leaf growth in spring.

Pincushion Hakea usually grows as a small tree 4–6 m (13–20 ft) tall. It can sometimes be taller, but rapid growth should not be encouraged by the frequent use of fertilisers as plants that develop too quickly can become unstable and be blown over, particularly if the soil becomes seasonally wet or waterlogged.

Hakea laurina likes fairly well-drained soils in a situation with full or partial sun. Plants are moderately frost-tolerant, but heavy frosts can cause damage to the flower-buds.

Hakea laurina

Hakea francisiana

Hardenbergia violacea NATIVE SARSAPARILLA

Purple is a wonderful flower colour in the garden and it is also an eye-catching part of the Australian bush. It is a colour that can be used in so many different ways. Vivid, bright combinations and contrasts can be achieved and purple can also be used to great effect in combination with white, creams and the softer, more subtle flower colours.

Native Sarsaparilla, sometimes also known as False Sarsaparilla, is a spreading groundcover, twining or climbing plant that can be found in Queensland, New South Wales, Victoria, Tasmania and South Australia. During winter and spring it provides a delightful display of small purple pea-flowers in sprays 10–20 cm (4–8 in) long.

This *Hardenbergia* is tolerant of a wide range of conditions in cultivation. It likes well-drained, acidic soils and a fairly sunny situation, but will do well in partial or filtered sunshine. Plants are useful as groundcovers beneath other shrubs or they can be allowed to twine through established plants to provide greater density of foliage and an additional display of colourful flowers. They are excellent for embankment planting and will help prevent soil erosion on steep slopes.

There are a number of different forms, including selections with white, pink or mauve flowers and some plants that are of shrubby habit.

Hardenbergia violacea 'Happy Wanderer' is an extremely vigorous climber with large sprays of purple flowers. This selection should be given adequate space to develop to its full potential in the garden; otherwise it will require regular pruning.

Hardenbergia violacea

Hibbertia empetrifolia　　SCRAMBLING GUINEA FLOWER

The genus *Hibbertia* generally has the common name of Guinea Flower, because of the rounded, golden flowers seen on almost all the 150 or more species. Some hibbertias produce scattered flowers right throughout the year but most remain relatively unnoticed in their natural habitat or in the garden until they come into bloom, when they light up the surrounding area with their showy display of bright golden-yellow. Most species are mat-forming groundcovers or small to medium shrubs, with a small number being of twining or climbing habit.

Hibbertia empetrifolia is a groundcover or climbing plant with reddish new stems and small, slightly rasp-like leaves. Its main flowering period is during spring, when there is a profuse display of small, bright yellow, open-petalled flowers.

The Scrambling Guinea Flower will grow in full sun or almost total shade and in well-drained or fairly moist, acidic soils. It will grow through shrubby plants, usually without smothering them or otherwise hindering their growth, and is extremely colourful when in flower. Plants respond well to pruning and clipping and are well worth a place in any garden. They are suitable also for containers or hanging baskets.

Hibbertia empetrifolia

91

Hymenosporum flavum   NATIVE FRANGIPANI

This *Hymenosporum* stands alone in the world of botany, as there is only a single species. It grows naturally in Queensland, New South Wales and New Guinea. Plants are adaptable in cultivation and will grow well and flower profusely in warm or cooler climates.

Flowers apart, *Hymenosporum flavum* is well worth growing as a delightful small to medium tree with glossy mid-green to dark green leaves. During spring to early summer its true value can be appreciated when the wonderful frangipani fragrance of the cream flowers begins to permeate the surroundings. The flowers are tubular with five spreading lobes at the tip and as they age their cream colour deepens to a rich yellow then burnt orange. The fragrance can be appreciated throughout the day, but is at its peak during the evening when plants attract small moths and other pollinating insects to the blooms.

The Native Frangipani will grow in a wide range of moist but well-drained soils, in a situation with full sun, filtered sun or sun for just part of the day. Plants can be damaged by heavy frost, particularly when very young. They respond well to light or heavy pruning and this can encourage the development of bushy growth and flowers at a lower level, where their beauty and fragrance can be appreciated to the maximum.

This is certainly a tree worthy of a place in gardens of either Australian or introduced plants. There are some dwarf selections now available but their eventual size and flower production under different conditions is still being evaluated.

Hymenosporum flavum

Hypocalymma angustifolium **WHITE MYRTLE**

Hypocalymma is a member of the Australian myrtle family, occurring in south-western Western Australia. White Myrtle is one of several Australian native plants with white flowers that age to pink or red. The result is an attractive combination of white and pink during the major part of the flowering season. The flowers are not large and dramatic but they are profuse. The flowering season is quite long, often extending from mid-winter through to early summer.

Hypocalymma angustifolium is a small to medium shrub 50 cm–2 m (1½–7 ft) tall by a similar width. The leaves are small and narrow, allowing the flowers to be well displayed along the branches. The young stem growth can be quite red, providing a further decorative feature.

Plants like moist, well-drained soils but are able to tolerate wet conditions for limited periods. They prefer a situation with partial or filtered sunlight, with at least some warmth and sunshine being desirable for good flower production.

White Myrtle responds well to pruning or picking and is grown commercially for cut-flower production. In the garden it combines very attractively with other plants that have pink to mauve flowers. The smaller forms, often available as 'Compact Selections', can also be grown with success in medium to large containers.

Hypocalymma angustifolium

93

Isopogon latifolius　　**BROAD-LEAVED ISOPOGON**

This is a showy shrub, also popular as a commercial cut-flower. The flower-heads, produced at the ends of the branches, are about 8 cm (3 in) across and are a rich purplish pink tipped with orange. They are produced mainly during spring to early summer.

There are about 35 *Isopogon* species, all occurring in Australia. Some are known by the common names of Cone Bush or Drumsticks, because of their globular, greyish, softly hairy seed-heads.

Isopogon latifolius grows naturally in south-western Western Australia, in well-drained sandy soils. It must have excellent drainage in cultivation and grows best in a sunny situation. Plants are usually bushy, growing 1–3 m (3¼–10 ft) tall, and they respond well to pruning or to the picking of the flowering stems.

Broad-leaved Isopogon offers a challenge to some gardeners as it does not have a high degree of adaptability to shaded situations or heavy, moist soils, but if your garden is sunny and with well-drained acidic soils it is certainly worthy of inclusion. Once established, plants usually grow well without regular watering or fertilising. They can react adversely to the use of fertilisers with a high phosphorus content.

Isopogon latifolius

Ixodia achilleoides MOUNTAIN DAISY

Mountain Daisy is a species perhaps best known as a superb cut-flower. It is also well worth growing for its beauty in the garden.

Plants flower mainly in spring to summer but some selections can bloom at other times. Very small, white everlasting daisies are produced in clusters at the ends of the stems and these can last for several years indoors as cut dried flowers, without any special treatment to preserve their beauty. If the flowers are heavy and the stalks slender the stems can be hung upside down to dry, to ensure that the stalks remain straight. Mountain Daisy is used extensively as a fresh or dried cut-flower, both in Australia and overseas. The flowers also respond well to dyeing and are frequently available in a wide range of colours.

Ixodia achilleoides is a small shrub with different forms varying in height from about 20 cm–1 m (8–40 in) tall. In nature it occurs in Victoria and South Australia. Plants like well-drained soils and a sunny situation for best results. They respond well to pruning or the picking of flowering stems. Some forms are not long-lived in cultivation, but they are still well worth growing and they can be readily propagated from cuttings if you wish to ensure a continuing supply of plants in the garden.

Ixodia achilleoides

95

Kunzea baxteri CRIMSON KUNZEA

Crimson Kunzea is somewhat similar in appearance to bright red *Callistemon* bottlebrushes when in flower, but with a distinctive brilliance that sets it apart from most other plants. It flowers mainly in autumn to early spring, with showy deep red brushes up to 10 cm (4 in) long, tipped with bright golden anthers.

There are over 30 species in the genus *Kunzea*, all native to Australia, with the majority occurring in south-western Western Australia.

Kunzea baxteri usually grows as a shrub 1.5–4 m (5–13 ft) tall. It has small, soft, light to mid-green leaves and plants can be densely foliaged, particularly if lightly pruned each year after flowering. Plants like a well-drained situation and do particularly well in sandy soils. They flower best in a sunny spot but will tolerate partial shade.

Some patience is needed before the first flowers appear: from seedling plants this can take up to ten years. Plants propagated from cuttings usually flower at an earlier age. It is often said that 'good things come to those who wait', and Crimson Kunzea is certainly worth the wait.

A grey-foliaged selection of this *Kunzea* is very attractive, as is the closely related *Kunzea pulchella* (Granite Kunzea).

Kunzea baxteri

Lambertia formosa   MOUNTAIN DEVIL

The genus *Lambertia* has 11 species, all native to Western Australia with the exception of *Lambertia formosa*, which occurs in New South Wales. The common name Honeysuckle is used in reference to many of the western species, as all *Lambertia* flowers are rich in nectar and are consequently an excellent source of food for native birds.

There is perhaps more than one reason why the common name Mountain Devil has been given to this attractive garden shrub. Firstly the fairly short green leaves have a sharply pointed tip, making it very useful for foot traffic control in the garden, whether those feet belong to adults, children or four-footed domestic pets; but is not an ideal plant for growing too close to a pathway. It is an excellent habitat plant for small birds. The second and more widely accepted reason for the common name refers to the intriguing shape of the woody fruits which, without needing much imagination at all, can be seen to strongly resemble a devil's head.

Lambertia formosa is a shrub 1.5–3 m (5–10 ft) tall, usually with a fairly upright growth habit. Plants respond well to pruning and can be used for hedging.

Mountain Devil can flower sporadically throughout the year but the peak flowering is usually spring to summer. Tubular red to orange–red flowers are produced in clusters of seven, surrounded by reddish bracts, at the ends of short branchlets. The woody devil-shaped fruits are about 2 cm (¾ in) long and each splits between the 'horns' to release two small seeds. These fruits are used for a range of novelty craft purposes, particularly in areas where the plants grow naturally. They do of course also add special interest to a garden, for both children and adults.

Lambertia formosa

Lechenaultia   LECHENAULTIAS

Lechenaultias have been named in honour of a nineteenth-century French naturalist and, despite its length, the botanical name is also fairly well known as the common name for the genus. There are 26 different lechenaultias, with the majority occurring in Western Australia.

Lechenaultia biloba (Blue Lechenaultia) is perhaps the best known species as it is renowned as being one of the most beautiful of all the world's blue flowers. The flowers, produced mainly from winter to early summer, are usually pale blue through to rich deep blue. Then there are a couple of unusual selections that have mauve–blue or white flowers.

Blue Lechenaultia is a low, lightly woody shrub, with slender branches, usually growing up to 50 cm (20 in) tall and spreading to a similar width.

Lechenaultia biloba is not regarded as a long-lived garden plant, but it is still well worth growing, even if treated as an annual or biennial. It does not usually self-seed in gardens, but new plants can be fairly readily propagated from cuttings. Some selections sucker lightly under favourable conditions and this usually increases the longevity of plants. A well-drained situation with a sunny or semi-shaded aspect is important for successful cultivation. Plants are also well suited to growing in containers. Pruning after flowering each year is strongly recommended to avoid plants developing leggy and brittle growth.

Lechenaultia biloba

Lechenaultia formosa is also extremely popular in cultivation. There are several forms of this species, sometimes known as the Red Lechenaultia, with flower colours that include yellow, orange, pinks and reds in numerous vivid and showy combinations. Flowering is mainly during winter and spring. Plants can be prostrate or up to 50 cm (20 in) tall, with the more upright selections being easier to grow than the prostrate ground-covering forms. Well-drained soils and a sunny situation are also important for the successful cultivation of this showy lechenaultia (see illustration on page 16).

Leptospermum rotundifolium 'Jervis Bay'
ROUND-LEAF TEA-TREE

The Round-leaf Tea-tree is a variable species, with several different flower-colour forms including white, pale to deep pink, or purplish pink. This particular selection from Jervis Bay on the coast of New South Wales has very attractive flowers of pink with a bluish purple tinge, seen mainly during spring to early summer.

Plants grow 2–3 m (6½–10 ft) tall and are of relatively upright habit with small, rounded, deep green leaves. They respond well to pruning, which helps to promote bushy growth.

Keep an eye out for some of the other selections of *Leptospermum rotundifolium*, which are also well worth growing; for example *Leptospermum rotundifolium* 'Lavender Queen' is a superb shrub, with large pale mauve–pink flowers.

There are about 80 *Leptospermum* species, most of which occur in Australia, but some are found in New Guinea, New Zealand and Southeast Asia. Most are reliable and adaptable plants in cultivation, able to tolerate moist or well-drained soils and suitable for full sun or fairly shaded situations.

The common name Tea-tree was used initially by members of Captain James Cook's voyage to Australia, who used *Leptospermum* leaves as a substitute for tea. The name Ti-tree is used in the Pacific islands in relation to paper-barked *Melaleuca* species. The product called tea-tree oil (or ti-tree oil) is made not from a *Leptospermum*, but from the oil of *Melaleuca alternifolia*, which is native to Queensland and New South Wales.

Leptospermum rotundifolium 'Jervis Bay'

Melaleuca HONEY-MYRTLES, PAPERBARKS

Melaleuca is a very large genus of plants with over 200 species. Nearly all occur only in Australia, where they are found in all States.

Some are low, spreading shrubs, others are tall trees and in between there are numerous small to tall shrubs that are showy and adaptable garden plants.

The common name Honey-myrtle refers to the often nectar-rich, sweetly scented flowers and the fact that this genus belongs to the myrtle family, Myrtaceae. Paperbark is the name given to many of the small to tall trees that have numerous thin layers of soft whitish to grey or tan bark. Not all species have bark of this type, but it is certainly a decorative and distinctive feature of those that do.

Most melaleucas grow well in situations with good drainage and full or partial sun, but there are some that tolerate almost total shade or extended periods of waterlogging, or both these conditions together. It is therefore important to check the requirements of each species if you are to grow plants in their preferred situations.

Melaleuca fulgens (Scarlet Honey-myrtle) is an attractive shrub 1–3 m (3¼–10 ft) tall with scarlet, pinkish red or salmon to apricot flowers in bottlebrush spikes about 5 cm (2 in) long. The flowering period is mainly spring to early summer. This species occurs in south-western Western Australia, but it adapts well in cultivation, preferring a sunny, well-drained situation.

Pruning from an early age is recommended to develop a good basic framework for plants and to encourage bushy growth. The salmon-flowered selection of this species is popular in cultivation as it provides an attractive colour not common in other flowers.

Melaleuca fulgens

Melaleuca lateritia (Robin Red-breast Bush) has flowers that aptly reflect the plant's common name. The flower-spikes produced from spring through to autumn are very similar in colour to the vivid breast of the Scarlet Robin. Robin Red-Breast Bush is a narrow-leaved shrub, usually 1.5–3.5 m (5–12 ft) tall. It is found naturally in Western Australia but is adaptable to a wide range of conditions in cultivation. Plants prefer full sun or semi-shade but will tolerate a fairly shaded site. They can also be grown in moist or well-drained soils and will tolerate limited periods of waterlogging. Plants can be frost-tender, particularly when young.

The flowers on the Robin Red-breast Bush are not usually as profuse as the bottlebrushes of *Callistemon* species, but they are as vivid and eye-catching, and *Melaleuca lateritia* is a very useful small screening shrub, even when not in bloom. Plants respond well to pruning and clipping.

Melaleuca lateritia

Melaleuca linariifolia (Snow in Summer), from Queensland and New South Wales, is grown as a street tree throughout much of Australia, where it usually develops to about 6 m (20 ft) tall, although it can become taller after many years. The trunk has papery bark and narrow, pointed, dark green leaves up to 3 cm (1 in) long. For between four and six weeks during spring and summer the foliage can be literally covered by the massed display of white to cream, somewhat feathery flowers. Plants are adaptable to a wide range of soil and climatic conditions.

Melaleuca linariifolia

Melaleuca nesophila (Showy Honey-myrtle) is another hardy and adaptable *Melaleuca* that can provide an excellent floral display during summer. It can grow as a shrub about 2 m (6½ ft) tall, while some forms develop as small trees with a height of about 6 m (20 ft). The bright green leaves are oblong and up to 4 cm (1½ in) long.

During spring and summer mauve to purple flowers tipped with gold are produced in globular heads to about 3 cm (1 in) across. They last well as cut-flowers but are not widely used commercially for this purpose.

Showy Honey-myrtle likes a sunny, well-drained situation but will also do well in partial or filtered sun. All forms respond well to pruning or clipping and are excellent screen or windbreak plants. They are useful for exposed coastal situations, but appreciate some protection from frosts, particularly when young.

Melaleuca nesophila

Olearia phlogopappa DUSTY DAISY-BUSH

The daisy family is one of the largest groups of the world's flowering plants. They are widely distributed throughout the world, with many being popular in cultivation.

Olearia is a genus of just under 200 species, the majority of which are found only in Australia. Most daisy plants are herbaceous or non-woody, but olearias are usually woody plants, giving rise to the common name of Daisy Bush. *Olearia argophylla,* from New South Wales, Victoria and Tasmania, can grow to a tree of 10 m (33 ft) or so in height, and is the world's largest daisy plant. It has an attractive timber that can be used for woodworking crafts.

Olearia phlogopappa is a shrubby plant 1–2 m (40–80 in) tall with green to greyish green leaves 1–5 cm (¼–2 in) long. During spring to late summer small daisy flowers are produced at the ends of the branchlets, often providing a very showy display. Various colour forms are obtainable including white, pink, mauve, bluish purple or blue, all with yellow centres.

Dusty Daisy-bush occurs in New South Wales, Victoria and Tasmania, usually in situations with filtered or partial sun. It does best in moisture-retaining but well-drained acidic soils. Plants respond extremely well to regular light pruning, right from the time of planting; this encourages a bushy framework. As they become established, pruning after flowering is recommended for continued good vigour and to avoid the development of sparse, leggy growth. The flowers last well indoors, and the cutting of flowering stems is an excellent form of pruning.

Olearia species are excellent for attracting butterflies to the garden.

A group planting of different forms of Dusty Daisy-bush can give a stunning effect, the white-flowered selection making a lovely combination with the pink or bluish forms.

Olearia phlogopappa

Orthrosanthus multiflorus **MORNING FLAG**

Numerous powder-blue flowers on upright stems to 1 m (40 in) tall, swaying in the breeze on a sunny day, make this plant a favourite of many plant enthusiasts.

Orthrosanthus is a genus of tuft-forming plants, belonging to the iris family. There are a total of seven species, four of which occur in Australia and three in South America.

Orthrosanthus multiflorus is well-named, with *multiflorus* literally meaning 'many flowers'. The flowering period is during spring. Although each flower lasts only a short time, flowering is continuous over many weeks.

Morning Flag can be grown in situations with partial sun, filtered sun or full open sunshine. It prefers soils that are moist for most of the year but with relatively good drainage. Plants are able to tolerate periods of drought or waterlogging as well as exposed coastal conditions and moderate frosts.

Plants with a tufting, grass-like habit are able to add a very special beauty to our gardens, which often consist primarily of shrubs and other non-grass-like species. If you feel an area of your garden is lacking something, and can't quite work out what it might be, try picturing the addition of a plant with grass-like foliage and erect spikes of pale blue flowers in spring. *Orthrosanthus multiflorus* may be just the plant to provide that spark of magic.

Orthrosanthus multiflorus

105

Pandorea jasminoides BOWER CLIMBER

Australia has many attractive native climbing plants, including six in the genus *Pandorea*.

Pandorea jasminoides is a popular garden plant, with several different forms. It is usually a strong climber or if no support is available it will grow as a spreading and scrambling groundcover. The main flowering period is between early spring and mid-autumn, when tubular flowers with flared tips, to about 5 cm (2 in) long by a similar width, provide a showy display. The flowering can be sporadic over a long period, or sometimes profuse and eye-catching.

Bower Climber occurs naturally in Queensland and New South Wales. The flowers, produced in sprays of up to ten flowers, are commonly pink with a reddish pink hairy throat. A number of selected colour variants are also obtainable, including 'Alba' and 'Lady Di', both with white flowers, 'Southern Belle' with pale pink flowers and 'Deep Pink' in which the flowers have a rich purplish pink colour. 'Charisma' is a pale pink selection with variegated green and cream foliage.

Pandorea jasminoides likes a fairly sunny situation with moist to well-drained soils. Plants respond well to pruning, and this may be desirable in some situations to restrict their growth.

Pandoreas are evergreen climbers and therefore very useful in a range of garden situations. The smaller-flowered *Pandorea pandorana* has many variants that flower profusely and these are also excellent climbers.

Pandorea jasminoides

Persoonia pinifolia   PINE-LEAVED GEEBUNG

There are over 50 species in the genus *Persoonia*, with one from New Zealand and the remainder occurring only in Australia.

Persoonias vary in habit from low groundcover shrubs to trees about 10 m (33 ft) tall. Nearly all have yellowish flowers, varying from deep cream to rich orange–yellow.

Persoonia pinifolia, from Queensland and New South Wales, is an attractive shrub 3–5 m (10–16½ ft) tall, and it is becoming increasingly popular as a garden plant. Its slender, narrow, non-prickly green leaves, about 6 cm (2¼ in) long, give rise to the species name *pinifolia* and common name Pine-leaved Geebung.

From summer through to early winter plants are adorned with continually lengthening sprays of small yellow flowers, providing a most attractive display. The flowers are then followed by clusters of fleshy, succulent fruits, causing the branchlets to droop with their weight. These fruits, which have a hard stone in the centre, are known as geebungs and used as a food source by Australian Aborigines.

Persoonia pinifolia needs well-drained soils and a fairly sunny situation for best results. Plants respond well to pruning, which encourages bushy growth. This plant may be a little difficult to find in nurseries, not because of lack of demand, but because it is not easy to grow using current methods of seed or cutting propagation. Plants are usually obtainable through specialist Australian plant nurseries, so if you see one and have space for a medium to large shrub, grab it while you can. You will find it truly delightful.

Persoonia pinifolia

Pimelea ferruginea RICE-FLOWER

Pimelea ferruginea has been grown in Australian gardens for many years, and when we consider its beauty as a small evergreen shrub it is easy to see why it is so popular.

There are about 100 species of *Pimelea*, occurring mainly in Australia with a small number from New Zealand. They are mainly low herbs and small to medium-size shrubs. Many are known by the common name Rice-flower, or simply as pimeleas.

Pimelea ferruginea, from Western Australia, is a shrub 50 cm–1.5 m (1½–5 ft) tall by a similar width. It has small, opposite, glossy green leaves and usually a naturally dense and rounded habit. Pruning each year after flowering certainly helps to maintain its bushy and attractive form.

During spring the foliage can be almost covered by the showy display of pale to deep pink flower clusters, produced at the ends of the branchlets.

Plants like a well-drained situation in full or partial sun. Once established they will tolerate exposed coastal situations, moderate frosts and soils that are seasonally quite dry.

A number of selected forms are obtainable including *Pimelea ferruginea* 'Bon Petite', which has deep pink flowers, 'Magenta Mist' with deep purplish pink flowers, and 'Pink Bouquet', which has deep pink flowers and variegated foliage. The flowers last relatively well indoors and are sometimes included in florists' bouquets.

Pimelea ferruginea

Prostanthera ovalifolia OVAL-LEAF MINT-BUSH

This is another extremely eye-catching shrub when in full bloom and it can't help but be noticed with its almost solid mass of bright purple flowers.

There are numerous Australian mint-bushes, many of which are popular in cultivation, making it difficult to choose just one for inclusion here. They have a great deal to offer, with most having pleasantly aromatic foliage and a profuse display of usually white, cream, pink, mauve or purple flowers, seen mainly during spring to early summer.

Prostanthera ovalifolia, from Queensland and New South Wales, is the species that has perhaps been the most commonly cultivated for a large number of years. Plants grow 2–4 m (6½–13 ft) tall, but they respond extremely well to regular pruning, which maintains bushy growth and encourages continued vigour. The softly toothed, oval leaves are green to greyish green, with a pleasant mint-like fragrance. Selections with variegated foliage are also obtainable. The main flowering time for this species is spring to early summer. Although the flowers are commonly bright purple, selections with pink or white flowers are also sometimes available.

Oval-leaf Mint-bush grows best in a moist but well-drained situation with partial or filtered sun. Plants can be grown successfully in full open sunshine, but generally those in a more sheltered location have a much longer life and can give many years of delight with their fragrance and beauty.

Prostanthera ovalifolia

Pultenaea pedunculata   MAT BUSH-PEA

The pea family is another extremely large, world-wide plant group. *Pultenaea* is an Australian native genus with over 100 species. They are mostly spreading groundcovers or small to medium shrubs, usually with a profuse display of yellow with orange, red or brownish flowers during spring to early summer. Some are also known by the general common name of Eggs-and-bacon.

Pultenaea pedunculata is a densely foliaged mat plant that spreads 1–2 m (40–80 in) across. It occurs naturally in New South Wales, Victoria, Tasmania and South Australia. During spring to early summer plants bear a profuse display of tiny pea-flowers, commonly yellow with a red centre. Selections of different colour forms are also now available, including plants with deep orange flowers; 'Pyalong Gold', which has all-yellow flowers; and 'Pyalong Pink', which has a showy display of soft pink flowers. See illustration on page 128.

Mat Bush-pea is an excellent groundcover amongst rocks and boulders, for hanging down embankments or retaining walls, or for general garden

use. It likes fairly well-drained soils and grows well in full or partial sun. Plants will usually remain densely foliaged without regular pruning but they respond well to cutting, which may be required if they are growing in restricted areas such as next to a pathway.

Mat Bush-pea can be used as a groundcover where there are no other plants in the area, or it is also quite happy to grow and spread among dwarf to small shrubs without smothering them or being detrimental to their growth. It will act as a living mulch and provide a protected root area for other plants that might benefit from this protection during summer. It can also be grown with success in containers or hanging baskets.

Pultenaea pedunculata

Rhodanthe chlorocephala subspecies *rosea*   **PINK EVERLASTING**

Until recently this delightful annual everlasting daisy was known as *Helipterum roseum*. It occurs naturally in Western Australia and from late winter to mid-summer can cover wide areas with a tall carpet of pink and white blooms.

This is a plant widely cultivated for the fresh and dried cut-flower market, both in Australia and overseas. It is also a very showy garden annual. A sunny situation is important for good results.

Pink Everlasting grows readily from seed, which should be planted from autumn through to early spring, with germination occurring 1–3 weeks from planting. It is important to protect young seedlings from slugs and snails. Plants can grow 15–70 cm (6–28 in) tall, but early pruning will encourage bushy growth and a greater number of flowers. Like other annuals, young plants are quick-growing and therefore need adequate moisture and nutrients to enable good development during their main growth period. Picking of the flowers as soon as they open will result in further blooms forming and the cut flowers can be used fresh or hung upside down to dry for prolonged use later.

Plants may self-seed in favourable garden conditions, or some of the daisies can be left on the plants until the seeds are fully mature, when they can be collected and stored in a dry location for re-planting next season.

The Pink Everlasting, sometimes also known as Rosy Sunray, is excellent for planting in an open, sunny position, particularly if you have a new garden and are looking for an instant garden effect while other slower growing shrubs become established, or for interim cover

in a garden area that is being re-developed.

This species is usually available in a pot or punnet, like other garden annuals. Packets of seed are also obtainable.

Rhodanthe manglesii is closely related, with similar cultivation requirements. (See illustration on page 14.)

Rhodanthe chlorocephala subspecies *rosea*

Rhododendron lochiae   AUSTRALIAN RHODODENDRON

Most gardeners are familiar with the large and very popular genus *Rhododendron*, which has a wide natural distribution in many areas of the world. Until 1995 there was just one Australian species, *Rhododendron lochiae*, but recent botanical studies have revealed two separate species, the other now named *Rhododendron notiale*.

These rhododendrons occur on a limited number of mountain peaks in Queensland, where they thrive in warm, sheltered, rainforest situations.

Rhododendron lochiae has oval, shiny green leaves about 10 cm (4 in) long and young stems with an attractive reddish tinge. In garden situations it usually grows as a shrub about 1 m (40 in) tall by a similar width, but in nature plants can grow much larger, often by scrambling

Rhododendron lochiae

among other rainforest species. Waxy, red, bell-shaped flowers up to 5 cm (2 in) long are produced in late summer and autumn.

In the garden this rhododendron likes a warm situation, with shelter from full hot sun, harsh winds and frost. It will grow well in a large container. Excessive use of fertilisers can result in an abundance of good foliage but few flowers.

The closely related *Rhododendron notiale* has a more upright growth habit without the reddish tinge in the new stems. The flowers are pinkish red and the tube section has a distinct curve rather than being straight. Cultivation requirements are similar for both species.

These two Australian rhododendrons are closely related to other species from New Guinea and neighbouring islands. Numerous hybrids with *Rhododendron lochiae* as one of the parents have been produced and are becoming increasingly available in nurseries.

A *Rhododendron lochiae* hybrid seedling

Scaevola aemula 'Purple Fanfare' FAN FLOWER

Members of the genus *Scaevola* are all commonly known as Fan-flower because of the shape of the flowers. They are tubular near the base with a split up one side, and five petals that in most species have a fan-like formation. The flowers come in a range of different colours, the most common being mauve to rich purple, pink or white.

Scaevola aemula is a variable species with a wide distribution from eastern to western Australia and several different forms in cultivation. *Scaevola aemula* 'Purple Fanfare' is a cultivar of outstanding ornamental value, with a showy display of rich purple flowers with a creamy centre, produced during late spring to summer. It is usually a low ground-covering plant that can spread 1–2 m (40–80 in) in diameter. Plants are also excellent for containers and hanging baskets. The closely allied 'Royal Fanfare' has a slightly more upright growth habit.

Pruning from an early stage encourages bushy growth and prevents plants from becoming sparse towards the centre. They like a sunny situation and good drainage, but need soils that are not too dry, particularly during the flowering period when their moisture requirements are high.

Scaevola flowers last well indoors, although their colour can fade in low light. Picking of the flowering stems will help to encourage further new growth from lower nodes.

Scaevola aemula 'Purple Fanfare'

Stenocarpus sinuatus FIREWHEEL TREE

Firewheel Tree is a very appropriate name for this plant, which produces bright red flowers opening out in circular wheel-like formations about 10 cm (4 in) across, mainly from mid-summer to late autumn. It grows naturally in Queensland, New South Wales and New Guinea.

Plants usually grow 6–10 m (20–33 ft) tall in cultivation, but very old trees can become larger, particularly in warm climatic zones. They have decorative foliage with shiny, dark green, often deeply lobed leaves 20–40 cm (8–16 in) long.

The Firewheel Tree will grow and flower well in tropical and subtropical zones and also in cooler temperate areas if given a warm sunny situation. It prefers relatively well-drained soils.

Some patience is needed when growing this plant, as it can take ten years or longer for the initial flowering to occur. In the meantime it is attractive as an evergreen foliage tree, so if you are prepared to welcome the flowers as a bonus it is certainly well worth growing. Future generations of home owners and gardeners will be grateful that the tree was included in the landscape, and we in turn can appreciate some of the long-term garden projects undertaken by those who have gone before us. While there is often a need for instant gardens and immediate results this is one case in which we can plan for the future by including a Firewheel Tree for our own later enjoyment and for the pleasure of our children and grandchildren.

Stenocarpus sinuatus can be grown for several years as an indoor foliage plant, then transferred to the garden when it becomes too large for the container or situation indoors.

Stenocarpus sinuatus

Swainsona formosa   STURT'S DESERT PEA

When we see this spectacular flower, with its common name commemorating the explorer Charles Sturt, our thoughts often turn to the arid inland regions of Australia and the excitement that must have gripped those who first saw this magnificent plant growing on the sun-scorched soils. *Swainsona formosa* (previously known as *Clianthus formosus*) is the floral emblem of South Australia.

This is not a plant that will survive in every home garden, and even in regions where it does do well it is not always long-lived, but it is so spectacular that many gardeners are prepared to provide the conditions for its survival.

Sturt's Desert Pea must have a very well-drained situation, either in the garden or in a large container, and as much direct sunshine as possible. It is usually a short-term plant that flowers during its first season, and it is common for it to be grown as an annual. Plants can spread to 2 m (6½ ft) or more across, with soft, greyish green, divided leaves. Clusters of large, brilliant red pea-flowers are produced on short stems during winter, spring, summer and early autumn.

Sturt's Desert Pea is closely related to *Clianthus puniceus* from New Zealand, and it is often grafted onto the *Clianthus* rootstock for increased longevity. If growing plants from seed it is important to provide protection from slugs and snails, which can demolish young seedlings very quickly.

Swainsona formosa is perhaps most commonly grown as a container plant in areas not ideally suited to its needs. It must have a well-drained potting mix, and success has been achieved using self-watering pots with a reservoir of water in the base, as a large plant with numerous flowering stems can use in excess of 2 litres (0.4 gal) of water per day.

Swainsona formosa

Syzygium paniculatum MAGENTA CHERRY

Syzygium is a widespread genus of several hundred species, about 50 being native to Australia. They are mostly rainforest trees with common names that include Satinash and Lilly Pilly.

Syzygium paniculatum usually grows as a tree about 8 m (26 ft) tall, but it can become larger after many years. The evergreen leaves are a glossy dark green. White fluffy flowers are produced during summer to early autumn, followed by ovoid, fleshy, magenta or mauve–red fruits about 2.5 cm (¾ in) in diameter.

Magenta Cherry responds well to pruning and clipping. The new growth can be pink, reddish or bronze and is very attractive. Plants are cultivated in Australia and overseas, often as ornamental standards and topiary or bonsai specimens. They like moist but well–drained soils in a sunny or semi–shaded situation.

The nectar-rich flowers and fleshy fruits of Magenta Cherry provide food for a range of native birds. The fruits are also recognised as an Australian bush food and can be used to make tasty jams, tarts and pies.

Syzygium paniculatum

Telopea speciosissima NEW SOUTH WALES WARATAH

In the New South Wales Waratah we have another of the most spectacular of all Australian native flowers. It is the floral emblem of New South Wales.

Telopea is a genus of four species, distributed in New South Wales, Victoria and Tasmania. Most have red flowers, although rare plants have been discovered with white and yellow flowers and used as parent stock in propagation and breeding programs. A number of hybrids have also been developed in recent years in conjunction with the high interest in the Waratah for cut-flower production.

The New South Wales Waratah is a shrub 2–5 m (6½–16½ ft) tall with large, often toothed leaves up to 25 cm (10 in) long. During spring numerous small red flowers are produced in spectacular heads up to 15 cm (6 in) diameter, at the end of long erect stems. These flower-heads are in most forms surrounded by petal-like bracts, or the bracts can be small or absent.

Plants respond well to pruning or to the cutting of flowering stems as soon as the flowers begin to open fully; this encourages a greater number of flowers during the following year. They like well-drained soils rich in organic matter and therefore able to retain sufficient moisture for the needs of the plant. A sunny situation is best for good flower production and plants also like growing in the company of low-growing shrubs that protect the root area from full exposure to the hot sun.

Telopea speciosissima 'Wirrimbirra White' is a named selection with

Telopea speciosissima

greenish white buds that open to white flowers. It has similar cultivation requirements to the red-flowered forms. This form is extremely rare in its natural habitat but it may have been known by the Aborigines of New South Wales, as according to Aboriginal legend there was a time when all waratah flowers were white, until a bird flying over the plants was shot with an arrow, spilling blood onto the flowers, after which all waratah flowers were red.

A seedling hybrid of the two waratahs pictured below

Telopea speciosissima (red-flowered selection) planted with *Telopea speciosissima* 'Wirrimbirra White'

Templetonia retusa   COCKIES' TONGUES

This plant may not be as well known to readers as many of the others included here, but it is well worth growing, particularly if you have an exposed coastal situation or highly alkaline soils, where cultivation of other plants can be challenging and often frustrating.

There are about ten species of *Templetonia*, all native to Australia.

Templetonia retusa occurs in South Australia and Western Australia. It is a relatively upright, shrubby plant 1–2.5 m (3¼–8 ft) tall with green to greyish green foliage. During late autumn to spring there is a vivid display of pea-flowers, usually bright red. Some variation in flower colour does exist: forms with pink, white, yellow or apricot flowers are occasionally obtainable.

Plants like an open, sunny situation and relatively well-drained soils. They respond well to pruning, which encourages bushy growth. Plants can be pruned immediately after flowering, or by cutting stems when they are in full bloom, as they are excellent as cut-flowers.

Templetonia retusa

Tetratheca ciliata PINK BELLS

There are about 40 species of *Tetratheca*, all of which occur in Australia. The majority are low clump-forming plants and many have brightly coloured flowers in the pink to mauve–purple colour range.

Pink Bells would be a worthy addition to most gardens. It is a small clump-forming plant about 50 cm (20 in) tall and up to 1 m (40 in) across, with small deep green leaves and a showy display of usually mauve–pink pendent bell-like flowers from winter through to early summer. A white-flowered form is also obtainable and the two different flower-colour forms make a very attractive combination when grown in close proximity.

Tetratheca ciliata grows in Victoria, Tasmania and South Australia. It prefers a moist but well-drained situation with partial or full sun, and is well suited to cultivation in gardens or containers.

Plants respond well to pruning after flowering, or to the cutting of flowering stems, which is an excellent form of pruning. The flowers retain their colour well when pressed or dried.

Tetratheca ciliata

Thomasia grandiflora   LARGE-FLOWERED THOMASIA

The Australian genus *Thomasia* is not widely known but several of its 30 or more species are grown by native plant enthusiasts and many are freely flowering and very attractive.

Thomasia grandiflora occurs naturally in Western Australia and is a spreading shrub about 1 m (40 in) tall by a similar width. Its dark green leaves are up to 4 cm (1½ in) long, with an attractive wavy-edged margin.

The flowering period is spring to early summer, when pendent pink to mauve flowers are produced at the ends of the branchlets. They have a soft papery texture and exquisite crinkled patterning on the petal-like bracts. Their full beauty is realised mainly when looking up into the flowers, which means that beetles, worms and other ground-dwelling garden creatures possibly get the nicest view. Perhaps cultivation in a high hanging basket has something to offer.

This *Thomasia* likes a relatively well-drained situation in full or partial sun, and is suitable for cultivation in gardens or containers.

Pruning during or immediately after flowering is recommended. As soon as the flowering is finished plants begin producing next year's flowers and late pruning often removes the forming buds.

Thomasia grandiflora, foreground

Thryptomene saxicola   ROCK THRYPTOMENE

There are about 30 species of *Thryptomene*, all native to Australia. One of the best known is the white-flowered *Thryptomene calycina*, which occurs in the Grampians area of Victoria and is widely grown for the cut-flower industry, both in Australia and overseas.

Thryptomene saxicola is native to Western Australia and is an attractive pink-flowered shrub. Plants grow to about 1.5 m (5 ft) tall by a similar width, with softly arching stems and small deep green to greyish green leaves. From autumn to spring they have a profuse display of small pale pink to deep pink flowers. Plants respond well to pruning or to the picking of the flowering stems, which are excellent for indoor use; but their arching habit means that plants are not as widely grown for this purpose as the Grampians Thryptomene.

Rock Thryptomene likes well-drained soils and a situation with full or partial sun. It is extremely attractive when grown in conjunction with other softly coloured plants flowering at a similar time. These include species of *Epacris* (Heath) and *Eriostemon* (Wax Flower).

Thryptomene saxicola

Verticordia mitchelliana   RAPIER FEATHER-FLOWER

The colour combination of grey–green leaves and bright red flowers is quite common in the Australian bush. It can be a strikingly beautiful combination and Rapier Feather-flower certainly comes into this category.

There are about 40 species of *Verticordia,* all of which occur in Western Australia. Many have profuse and vivid flowers in a wide range of colours.

Verticordia mitchelliana is a shrub reaching 1 m (40 in) tall by a similar width. Its grey–green leaves are about 1 cm (¼ in) long and the flowers are at their peak during spring to summer.

Rapier Feather-flower is not regarded as an easy-to-grow plant as, like many other verticordias, it is quite specific in its requirements. It needs excellently drained soils and a warm to hot, sunny situation. Some species of *Verticordia* are now obtainable as grafted plants; this increases their adaptability in cultivation. The growing of plants in containers is another method of cultivation that can be helpful in providing the conditions most suited to their requirements.

Verticordias are eagerly sought as cut-flowers and many are equally beautiful fresh or dried. Research is therefore being undertaken in an effort to develop more success in propagating and cultivating members of this highly desirable group of plants.

Verticordia mitchelliana

Viola hederacea NATIVE VIOLET

Do you have a spot in the garden that rarely receives any direct sunshine, always seems slightly moist, and where you would like to be able to grow something other than ferns? The Australian Native Violet may be just what you have been looking for.

Viola hederacea is a delightful low groundcover that puts down roots from its creeping stems to form a lush, rich green cover in favourable conditions. Widespread in the eastern States, it can flower almost non-stop throughout the year, with a peak from spring through to autumn. The flowers, produced on slender upright stems, are usually purple and white. Selected forms are available with white flowers, and the flowers of 'Baby Blue' are a rich but soft blue to mauve–blue.

The Native Violet lacks the strong fragrance of the introduced *Viola odorata* but the flowers do have a soft, delicate perfume.

Native Violet is happy to scramble around other garden plants and if plants wander further than you wish, the surplus can simply be pulled up and discarded, or potted up and given away to friends.

Viola hederacea 'Baby Blue'

Xanthosia rotundifolia SOUTHERN CROSS

The Southern Cross is the well-known constellation featured on the Australian flag. It is the common name given to this extremely desirable native shrub because of the interesting and unusual formation of the attractive cream and pink flowers, which are actually quite small and surrounded by much larger, cream, petal-like bracts. Once plants become established in the garden they are rarely without some flowers right throughout the year, and there is usually a profuse display in late spring to early summer.

Xanthosia rotundifolia is a low, spreading to scrambling shrub about 30 cm (12 in) tall by 1–2 m (40–80 in) across. The dark green leaves are rounded, with a softly toothed margin. Regular pruning and removal of some of the oldest stems promotes new growth and continued flowering.

Southern Cross occurs naturally in south-western Western Australia. It is an adaptable plant that can be grown in a range of conditions. Plants prefer a moist but well-drained situation in acidic soils and will grow in full sun, partial sun or filtered shade.

Xanthosia rotundifolia